Learning Python Data Visualization

Master how to build dynamic HTML5-ready SVG charts using Python and the pygal library

Chad Adams

PUBLISHING

BIRMINGHAM - MUMBAI

Learning Python Data Visualization

First published: August 2014

Production reference: 1180814

Published by Packt Publishing Ltd.
Livery Place
35 Livery Street
Birmingham B3 2PB, UK.

ISBN 978-1-78355-333-4

www.packtpub.com

Cover image by Sabine Mehlstäubl (sabine@blumen-schmidl.de)

Credits

Author
Chad Adams

Reviewers
Aniket Maithani

Atmaram Shetye

Giuseppe Vettigli

Ron Zacharski

Commissioning Editor
Akram Hussain

Acquisition Editor
Joanne Fitzpatrick

Content Development Editor
Parita Khedekar

Technical Editor
Venu Manthena

Copy Editors
Janbal Dharmaraj

Insiya Morbiwala

Sayanee Mukherjee

Aditya Nair

Deepa Nambiar

Stuti Srivastava

Project Coordinator
Neha Thakur

Proofreaders
Simran Bhogal

Maria Gould

Ameesha Green

Indexers
Hemangini Bari

Tejal Soni

Priya Subramani

Production Coordinator
Shantanu Zagade

Cover Work
Shantanu Zagade

About the Author

Chad Adams is a web and mobile software developer based in Raymore, Missouri, where he works as a mobile frontend architect creating visually appealing application software for iOS, Windows Phone, and the Web. He also creates project build systems for large development teams using programming languages such as Python and C#. He has a B.F.A. in Commercial Art and a Microsoft certification in HTML5, JavaScript, and CSS3. He has also spoken at conferences on topics that include Windows Phone development and Google Dart. In his off hours, Chad enjoys relaxing at his home and spending time with his wife, Heather, and son, Leo.

About the Reviewers

Aniket Maithani is a budding engineer and is currently pursuing a B.Tech in Computer Science and Engineering from Amity University. He is primarily interested in contributing to open source projects and believes in the FOSS/FLOSS ideology. He has been working in the field of embedded systems and open hardware for the last two years. Apart from coding and hacking around with regular stuff, he loves to play the guitar and write on his blog. He can be reached at me@aniketmaithani.net.

There are a few people I would like to thank for helping me out. Firstly, my dad, who introduced me to the world of computers! Also, I would like to thank my professor Mr. Manoj Baliyan and my senior Mr. Anuvrat Parashar, who introduced me to the world of Python and its awesomeness. I would also like to thank my mentor, Satyakaam Goswami for always guiding me. Lastly, God Almighty for his kind grace and blessings.

Atmaram Shetye is a Computer Science and Engineering Graduate from Goa University. Having worked in a variety of companies, from start-ups to large multinational enterprises, he is a strong supporter of polyglot programming. He has spent most of his time programming in Python, while also using C, Objective-C, C++, and JavaScript at work. His areas of interest include artificial intelligence and machine learning. He is currently working as a Principal Software Engineer at CA Technologies, Bangalore.

Giuseppe Vettigli is a data scientist who has worked in the research industry and academia for many years. His work is focused on the development of machine learning models and applications to utilize information from structured and unstructured data. He also writes about scientific computing and data visualization in Python on his blog at `http://glowingpython.blogspot.com`.

Ron Zacharski completed a PhD in Computer Science at the University of Minnesota, focusing on artificial intelligence and computational linguistics. He is the author of the free online Python-based book, *A Programmer's Guide to Data Mining: The Ancient Art of the Numerati* (`http://www.guidetodatamining.com`). He is an Associate Professor of Computer Science at the University of Mary Washington. Ron is a novice Zen Buddhist monk.

www.PacktPub.com

Support files, eBooks, discount offers, and more

You might want to visit www.PacktPub.com for support files and downloads related to your book.

Did you know that Packt offers eBook versions of every book published, with PDF and ePub files available? You can upgrade to the eBook version at www.PacktPub.com and as a print book customer, you are entitled to a discount on the eBook copy. Get in touch with us at service@packtpub.com for more details.

At www.PacktPub.com, you can also read a collection of free technical articles, sign up for a range of free newsletters and receive exclusive discounts and offers on Packt books and eBooks.

http://PacktLib.PacktPub.com

Do you need instant solutions to your IT questions? PacktLib is Packt's online digital book library. Here, you can access, read and search across Packt's entire library of books.

Why subscribe?

- Fully searchable across every book published by Packt
- Copy and paste, print and bookmark content
- On demand and accessible via web browser

Free access for Packt account holders

If you have an account with Packt at www.PacktPub.com, you can use this to access PacktLib today and view nine entirely free books. Simply use your login credentials for immediate access.

Table of Contents

Preface	**1**
Chapter 1: Setting Up Your Development Environment	**7**
Introduction	**7**
Setting up Python on Windows	**7**
Installation	**9**
Exploring the Python installation in Windows	**15**
Python editors	**20**
Setting up Python on Mac OS X	**25**
Setting up Python on Ubuntu	**31**
Summary	**34**
Chapter 2: Python Refresher	**35**
Python basics	**35**
Importing modules and libraries	40
Input and output	42
Generating an image	45
Creating SVG graphics using svgwrite	**48**
For Windows users using VSPT	48
For Eclipse or other editors on Windows	50
For Eclipse on Mac and Linux	50
Summary	**59**
Chapter 3: Getting Started with pygal	**61**
Why use pygal?	**61**
Installing pygal using pip	64
Installing pygal using Python Tools for Visual Studio	66
Building a line chart	67
Stacked line charts	**69**
Simple bar charts	**71**

Stacked bar charts	**72**
Horizontal bar charts	**73**
XY charts	**74**
Scatter plots	**77**
DateY charts	**78**
Summary	**83**
Chapter 4: Advanced Charts	**85**
Pie charts	**85**
Stacked pie charts	86
Radar charts	**88**
Box plots	**89**
Dot charts	**91**
Funnel charts	**94**
Gauge charts	**96**
Pyramid charts	**98**
Worldmap charts	**101**
Summary	**104**
Chapter 5: Tweaking pygal	**105**
Country charts	**105**
Parameters	**108**
Legend at the bottom	109
Legend settings	111
Label settings	**116**
Chart title settings	**120**
Displaying no data	**123**
pygal themes	**124**
Summary	**126**
Chapter 6: Importing Dynamic Data	**127**
Pulling data from the Web	**127**
The XML refresher	**130**
RSS and the ATOM	**131**
Understanding HTTP	**131**
Using HTTP in Python	132
Parsing XML in Python with HTTP	**134**
About JSON	**136**
Parsing JSON in Python with HTTP	**136**
About JSONP	**143**
JSONP with Python	**144**
Summary	**144**

Chapter 7: Putting It All Together   145
Chart usage for a blog   145
Getting our data in order   146
Converting date strings to dates   149
Using strptime   150
Saving the output as a counted array   156
Counting the array   158
Python modules   160
Building the main method   161
Modifying our RSS to return values   162
Building our chart module   163
Building a portable configuration for our chart   164
Setting up our chart for data   165
Configuring our main function to pass data   167
Project improvements   168
Summary   170
Chapter 8: Further Resources   171
The matplotlib library   171
Installing the matplotlib library   172
matplotlib's library download page   173
Creating simple matplotlib charts   173
Plotly   179
Pyvot   186
Summary   187
Appendix: References and Resources   189
Links for help and support   189
Charting libraries   189
Editors and IDEs for Python   190
Other libraries and Python alternative shells   190
Index   191

Preface

Greetings, this is Chad Adams, and welcome to *Learning Python Data Visualization*. In this book, we will cover the basics of generating dynamic charts and general graphics with code using the Python programming language. We will use the pygal library, a simple yet powerful graphing library written for Python, to explore the different types of charts we can create for various kinds of data.

We will also review the Python language itself and discuss working with file I/O and cover topics on working with data. We will then parse that data into a chart to create a dynamic charting application. We will also touch on more popular (and more advanced) libraries such as matplotlib and Plotly and build charts using these libraries and explore their features.

With this book, we will explore and build data visualizations using the basic toolsets used in many popular charting applications for the scientific, financial, medical, and pharmaceutical industries.

What this book covers

Chapter 1, Setting Up Your Development Environment, will discuss the installation process for Python on Windows, Mac, and Ubuntu. We will review the easy_install and pip package managers for Python and discuss common issues when installing third-party libraries for Python.

Chapter 2, Python Refresher, will quickly review the Python language and common libraries found in most Python developers' tool belts. We will also ease into building charts by creating custom graphics with nothing but code and learn about saving files to the filesystem.

Chapter 3, Getting Started with pygal, will cover the basics of the pygal library, a simple charting library that generates charts in HTML5-ready SVG files. We will build some basic charts using the library, some of which include line charts, bar charts, and scatter plots.

Chapter 4, Advanced Charts, will cover more complex charts in the pygal library such as box plots, radar charts, and worldmap charts.

Chapter 5, Tweaking pygal, will discuss the optional settings we can give our pygal charts such as adjusting the font size and the positioning of labels and legends. We will also cover the French country map chart in the pygal library using it as an example.

Chapter 6, Importing Dynamic Data, will go over the finer points of pulling data from the Web using the Python language and its built-in libraries and cover parsing XML, JSON, and JSONP data.

Chapter 7, Putting It All Together, will build a simple chart that takes what we learned from the past chapters and builds a dynamic pygal-based chart using data from the Web.

Chapter 8, Further Resources, will review some very popular charting libraries such as matplotlib and Plotly, go over building sample charts for each library, and cover resources for further reading.

Appendix, References and Resources, will list some popular data visualization libraries for Python as well as some helpful utilities.

What you need for this book

You will need Windows, Mac, or an Ubuntu system that is running Python 2.7 32-bit or Python 2.7 64-bit. You will need to have administrator rights on this system. You will also need a Python text editor such as Eclipse or Visual Studio with Python Tools. For *Chapter 8, Further Resources,* you will also need Python 3.4 or higher. Python 2.7 and 3.4 can be installed alongside each other.

Who this book is for

If you're new to the Python language and are looking at getting into building charts using Python, this is a great resource to get started. If you have done a bit of Python development already but have not ventured into graphics and charts, there is plenty of information in this book with regards to creating these.

Conventions

In this book, you will find a number of styles of text that distinguish between different kinds of information. Here are some examples of these styles, and an explanation of their meaning.

Code words in text, database table names, folder names, filenames, file extensions, pathnames, dummy URLs, user input, and Twitter handles are shown as follows: "Create a text file called `PyREADME.txt` and save it to your project's directory."

A block of code is set as follows:

```
def main():
    print("Hello, World")
main()
```

Any command-line input or output is written as follows:

```
sudo pip install pygal
```

New terms and **important words** are shown in bold. Words that you see on the screen, in menus or dialog boxes for example, appear in the text like this: "Click on **OK** on both windows to save and reboot your PC again."

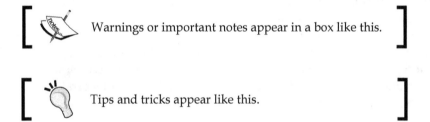

Warnings or important notes appear in a box like this.

Tips and tricks appear like this.

Reader feedback

Feedback from our readers is always welcome. Let us know what you think about this book — what you liked or may have disliked. Reader feedback is important for us to develop titles that you really get the most out of.

To send us general feedback, simply send an e-mail to `feedback@packtpub.com`, and mention the book title via the subject of your message.

If there is a topic that you have expertise in and you are interested in either writing or contributing to a book, see our author guide on www.packtpub.com/authors.

Customer support

Now that you are the proud owner of a Packt book, we have a number of things to help you to get the most from your purchase.

Downloading the example code

You can download the example code files for all Packt books you have purchased from your account at http://www.packtpub.com. If you purchased this book elsewhere, you can visit http://www.packtpub.com/support and register to have the files e-mailed directly to you.

Errata

Although we have taken every care to ensure the accuracy of our content, mistakes do happen. If you find a mistake in one of our books—maybe a mistake in the text or the code—we would be grateful if you would report this to us. By doing so, you can save other readers from frustration and help us improve subsequent versions of this book. If you find any errata, please report them by visiting http://www.packtpub.com/submit-errata, selecting your book, clicking on the **errata submission form** link, and entering the details of your errata. Once your errata are verified, your submission will be accepted and the errata will be uploaded on our website, or added to any list of existing errata, under the Errata section of that title. Any existing errata can be viewed by selecting your title from http://www.packtpub.com/support.

Piracy

Piracy of copyright material on the Internet is an ongoing problem across all media. At Packt, we take the protection of our copyright and licenses very seriously. If you come across any illegal copies of our works, in any form, on the Internet, please provide us with the location address or website name immediately so that we can pursue a remedy.

Please contact us at copyright@packtpub.com with a link to the suspected pirated material.

We appreciate your help in protecting our authors, and our ability to bring you valuable content.

Questions

You can contact us at questions@packtpub.com if you are having a problem with any aspect of the book, and we will do our best to address it.

1
Setting Up Your Development Environment

Introduction

In this chapter, we will review how to set up the Python 2.7 32-bit edition on Windows, Mac, and Ubuntu Linux. We will walk through the Python interpreter and build a few Hello-World-style Python applications to ensure our code is working properly. This will be covered primarily in the Windows section of the chapter, but it will be reiterated in other OS sections.

We will also review how to install and use **easy_install** and **pip**, which are package managers that are commonly used in Python development. We will also review how to install **lxml**, which is a popular xml parser and writer that we will need in later chapters.

Setting up Python on Windows

If you're fairly new to Python, you might have heard that Python doesn't have the right build tools to run on Windows or that Python is optimized for Unix-based systems such as Mac OS X and Linux variations. In part, this is true; most libraries, including ones that are covered in this book, work better and are easier to install if you are on an operating system that isn't Windows.

I want to spend a little extra time in this section in case you, the reader, want to use Windows as your development OS while working through this book. Firstly, I want to cover why Windows is known to have issues with Python developers. Typically, it's not the language that causes issues, and nor the lack of editors. In fact, Windows has even more high-quality editors for Python, including Visual Studio with Python Tools, and more text editor options such as Notepad++.

The real problem that plagues developers is library compatibility, specifically, Python libraries that reference C-based code to achieve results that are not possible using the Python language directly. Unlike Mac OS X or Linux variations, Windows does not include a C compiler as a part of the OS. Typically, when a Python library author mentions Windows's "lack of build tools", this usually refers to Windows not including a C compiler.

Another issue is the command prompt; it's typical in Python development to install libraries and assets using the terminal or using the command prompt in Windows commands. The two common commands to install libraries are `easy_install` and `pip`. If you're not familiar, easy_install is a command-line based package manager for Python. It uses Python eggs, (a renamed `.zip` file specific to easy_install) to bundle the scripts and required files for a library. The easy_install package manager is also an older package manager and has been in the Python tool belt for ages. It's typical to find older Python libraries using easy_install. The following screenshot shows you the PyPI website:

The other command, called pip, is also known as **Python Package Index (PyPi)**. Whereas easy_install has been community driven, PyPi is the official package manager of the Python Software Foundation, the group that is in charge of updates and taking care of the Python language. The site also hosts third-party packages.

The following screenshot shows you the Python website:

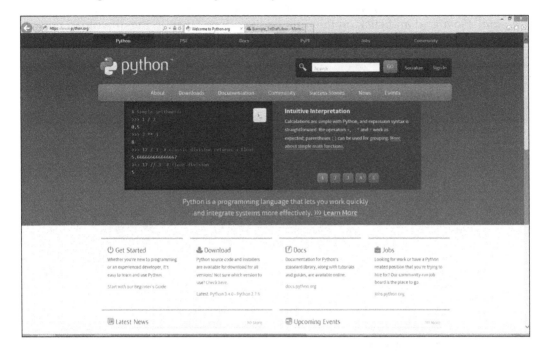

 Newer libraries are usually created using pip for two reasons. One, pip has more features than easy_install and two, pip libraries are searchable on Python's official package site repository at `https://pypi.python.org/pypi`.

Installation

Let's start with installing Python on your Windows machine. For this book, I'll be using Windows 8.1, though this workflow should be fine if you're running Windows 7 or Windows Vista. First, open up your browser of choice and navigate to `http://www.python.org/`.

On the home page, you should see a download link as shown in the preceding screenshot. For Windows, we are looking for Python Version 2.7+ (the 32-bit Version). Go ahead and click on that link and you'll be taken to the download page:

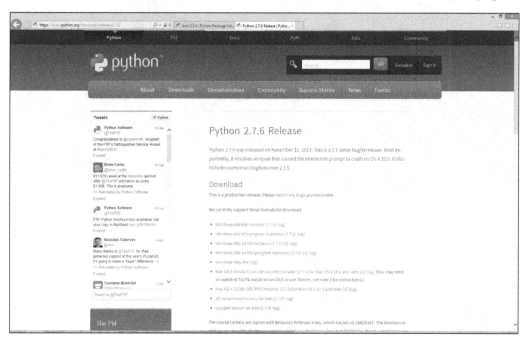

On the download page, you'll want to download the Windows x86 MSI installer. We want the 32-bit installer rather than the 64-bit installer. This will ensure optimal compatibility with packages in upcoming chapters. The following screenshot shows you the general installation window for Python on Windows (shown here with a 64-bit version of Python for demo purposes):

Once you've downloaded the installer, double-click on the installer to run it. Follow the wizard and leave the defaults alone, particularly the path where Python is installed as shown in the preceding screenshot. Let the installer work through the installation and reboot your system.

After rebooting your system, if you're in Windows 8 on the desktop tile, right-click on the **Start** screen icon and click on **System**. Then, click on **Advanced system settings** (if you're in Windows 7 or Vista, you can find this by navigating to **Control Panel | All Control Panel Items | System**), as shown in the following screenshot:

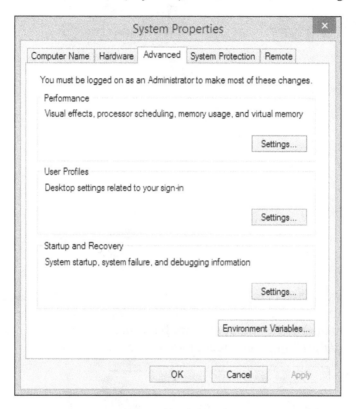

Once you've done that, you'll want to click on **Environment Variables**, as shown in the preceding screenshot, and look for **Path** under **System variables**. These variables allow the command prompt to know what programs it has access to anywhere in your system. We have to edit the **Path** as shown in the following screenshot, select **Path**, and click on **Edit**:

With the **Edit** menu visible, type `C:\Python27;C:\Python27\Lib\site-packages\;C:\Python27\Scripts\;` (including the semicolon at the front to differentiate paths) at the end of the variable value. Click on **OK** on both windows to save the changes and reboot your PC again.

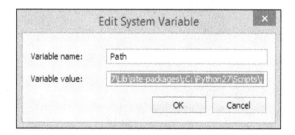

Now, let's test your Python installation! Open up your command prompt, and type `python` in lowercase and press *Enter*. Assuming the installer worked properly, you should see the command prompt path cursor location change to precede >>>, as shown in the following screenshot:

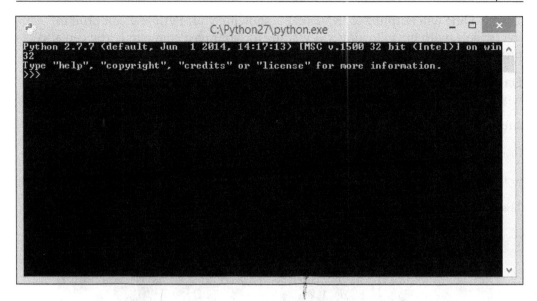

You are now in the Python interpreter; here, you can run simple one line scripts such as the following command:

```
print('Hello Reader!')
```

Downloading the example code

You can download the example code files for all Packt books you have purchased from your account at http://www.packtpub.com. If you purchased this book elsewhere, you can visit http://www.packtpub.com/support and register to have the files e-mailed directly to you.

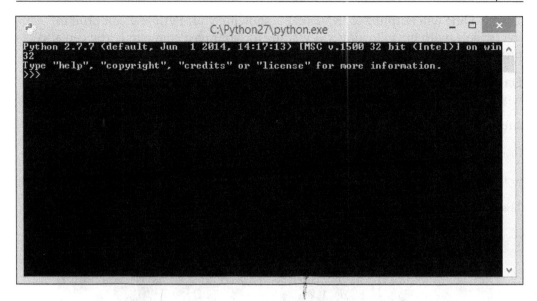

The next line will output `Hello Reader!`, showing your Python script print to the console, with the following >>> waiting for your next command. You can also process commands such as: `2 + 2`, hit *Enter*, and you will see `4` on the next line.

Let's try to save a variable to the prompt; type the following command on the next line:

```
authorsName = 'Chad'
```

Press *Enter*. Then, type the following command and press *Enter* again:

```
print(authorsName)
```

The output is shown in the next screenshot:

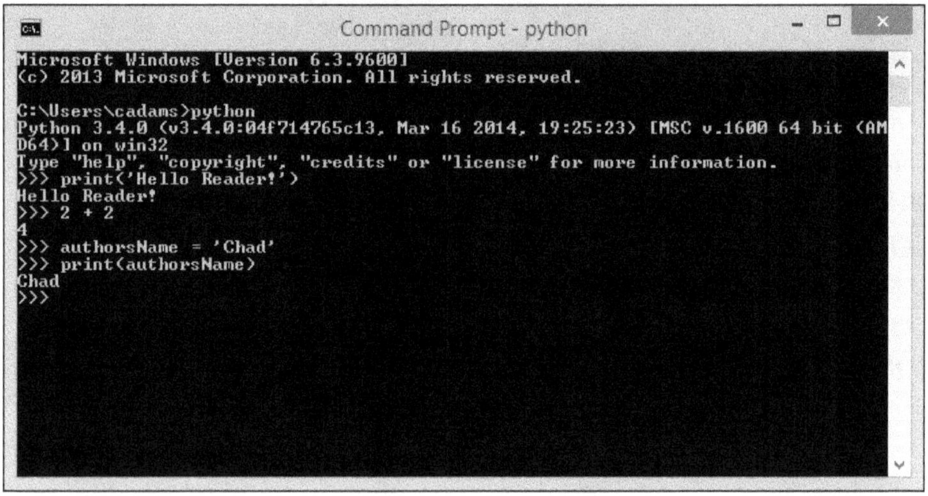

Now, your command prompt will look like the preceding screenshot. Notice on the resulting line that `Chad` is the output for the `authorsName` Python variable. This means that you've installed the Python compiler correctly! We've confirmed that Python works on Windows by testing the function object, the math object, and the variable objects.

With that tested, you can return to the standard command prompt from the Python compiler by exiting the compiler. Simply type `exit(0)` to exit the Python instance.

Exploring the Python installation in Windows

Now that we have reviewed the command line on Windows, we need to know a few other things before we start writing code. Let's start with where Python and any libraries are installed on your machine. Open Windows Explorer and navigate to C:\Python27, as shown in the following screenshot:

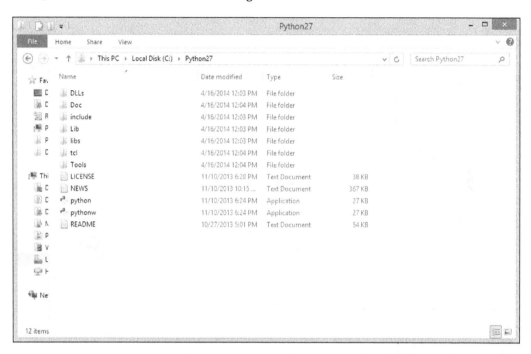

Inside the Python27 directory, you can see the python.exe file; this is the application that our **Path** in **System variables** looks for to run Python scripts and commands. This folder also contains other libraries that are to required be run by Python, including libraries downloaded from easy_install or pip.

You can find the third-party libraries by navigating to C:\Python27\Lib\site-packages. Any libraries and any third-party dependencies downloaded through pip or easy_install will be installed in this directory by default.

Next, let's pull down a few libraries we will need for this book. Python 2.7 on Windows pip and easy_install are included with Python's Windows Installer by default. First, we will need the `lxml` library. Now, on Windows, the `lxml` library is a very popular C-based XML parser and writer library for Python libraries and is notoriously incompatible with Windows systems due to its C-based implementation. Let's install the `lxml` library before pulling packages that might depend on this, staring with `lxml`, as shown in the following screenshot:

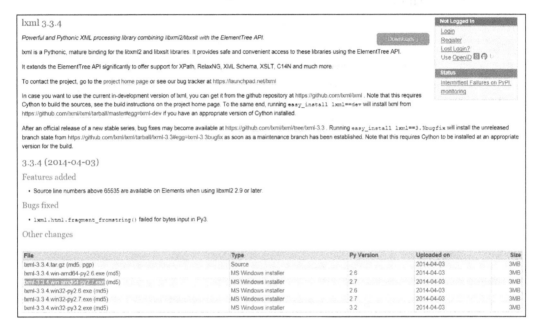

lxml does come in both pip and easy_install flavors; however, since it's C-based, we require the Windows installer found at `https://pypi.python.org/pypi/lxml/3.3.3`. Grab the `lxml-3.3.3.win32-py2.7.exe` file or a newer Version 2.7 library and run the installer. Once it's installed, we can confirm the installation by navigating to the `site-packages` directory and checking whether any new folder called `lxml` has been created. When installed, the `site-packages` directory should look like the following screenshot:

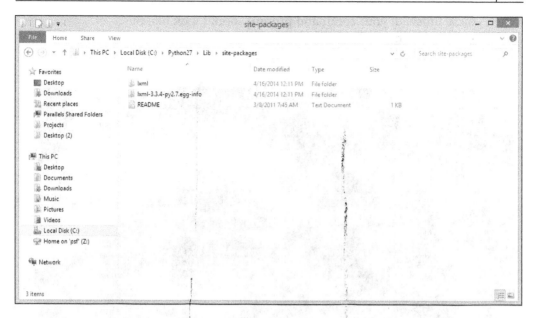

After `lxml` is installed, we will set up easy_install and pip. First, let's download easy_install and install it. The steps are as follows:

1. Navigate your browser of choice to `https://pypi.python.org/pypi/setuptools`.

2. Then, download the `ez_setup.py` file.

3. Save the file to `C:\Python27\ez_setup.py`. You can find the file on the page here, as shown in the following screenshot:

Installation Instructions

The recommended way to bootstrap setuptools on any system is to download ez_setup.py and run it using the target Python environment. Different operating systems have different recommended techniques to accomplish this basic routine, so below are some examples to get you started.

Setuptools requires Python 2.6 or later. To install setuptools on Python 2.4 or Python 2.5, use the bootstrap script for Setuptools 1.x.

The link provided to ez_setup.py is a bookmark to bootstrap script for the latest known stable release.

Now, open your command prompt again with administrator privileges, then type the following command, and press *Enter*:

```
cd c:\Python27
```

Next, type the following command and press *Enter*:

```
python ez_setup.py
```

When you're finished, your command prompt should look like the following screenshot:

Now, let's test easy_install and install pip at the same time! Again, open the command prompt and set your directory like you did previously:

```
cd c:\Python27
```

Then, type the following command and press *Enter*:

```
easy_install pip
```

If you're successful, your command prompt should look something like the following screenshot:

```
Command Prompt                                          _  □  ×
Processing pip-1.5.4.tar.gz
Writing c:\users\cadams\appdata\local\temp\easy_install-v66fp6\pip-1.5.4\setup.c
fg
Running pip-1.5.4\setup.py -q bdist_egg --dist-dir c:\users\cadams\appdata\local
\temp\easy_install-v66fp6\pip-1.5.4\egg-dist-tmp-bbcvb3
warning: no files found matching 'pip\cacert.pem'
warning: no files found matching '*.html' under directory 'docs'
warning: no previously-included files matching '*.rst' found under directory 'do
cs\_build'
no previously-included directories found matching 'docs\_build\_sources'
Adding pip 1.5.4 to easy-install.pth file
Installing pip-script.py script to C:\Python27\Scripts
Installing pip.exe script to C:\Python27\Scripts
Installing pip2.7-script.py script to C:\Python27\Scripts
Installing pip2.7.exe script to C:\Python27\Scripts
Installing pip2-script.py script to C:\Python27\Scripts
Installing pip2.exe script to C:\Python27\Scripts

Installed c:\python27\lib\site-packages\pip-1.5.4-py2.7.egg
Processing dependencies for pip
Finished processing dependencies for pip

C:\Python27>
```

With that done, let's test pip! We want to try to install a library called BeautifulSoup. It's a common Python library for scrapping HTML content. We won't be using BeautifulSoup but we need to test the pip installation, and BeautifulSoup is a good library that works with most installations. To install BeautifulSoup in your console while still it's open and the path is still pointing to your C:\Python27 directory, type the following command:

```
pip install beautifulsoup
```

You'll see a message at the end, as shown in the following screenshot:

```
Adding pip 1.5.4 to easy-install.pth file
Installing pip-script.py script to C:\Python27\Scripts
Installing pip.exe script to C:\Python27\Scripts
Installing pip2.7-script.py script to C:\Python27\Scripts
Installing pip2.7.exe script to C:\Python27\Scripts
Installing pip2-script.py script to C:\Python27\Scripts
Installing pip2.exe script to C:\Python27\Scripts

Installed c:\python27\lib\site-packages\pip-1.5.4-py2.7.egg
Processing dependencies for pip
Finished processing dependencies for pip

C:\Python27>pip install beautifulsoup
Downloading/unpacking beautifulsoup
  Downloading BeautifulSoup-3.2.1.tar.gz
  Running setup.py (path:c:\users\cadams\appdata\local\temp\pip_build_cadams\bea
utifulsoup\setup.py) egg_info for package beautifulsoup

Installing collected packages: beautifulsoup
  Running setup.py install for beautifulsoup

Successfully installed beautifulsoup
Cleaning up...

C:\Python27>
```

Python editors

We have now installed the necessary libraries and frameworks that are required to build Python scripts, so let's pick a code editor. For first-time (and even veteran Python) developers, I recommend an IDE as an editor of choice over a plain text editor. This is mainly for two reasons. One, an IDE typically includes code hinting of some kind to give the developer an idea of what Python packages are available or even installed on the developer's system. Two, most good IDEs include Python-specific code-documentation templates and helpers that help write large code bases.

One of the more popular IDEs is Eclipse with PyDev; it's free and is a very good starter IDE for Python. We will cover Eclipse in more depth in the next sections for other platforms, but if you intend to use Eclipse on Windows, be sure to install the latest Java runtime and JDK installers for your version of Windows. Read ahead to learn more about Eclipse with PyDev.

If you come from a .NET background or prefer Visual Studio in general, check out Python Tools for Visual Studio. This allows you to run Python code in a Visual Studio project and be able to keep Python code in Team Foundation Server (Microsoft's source control system). The following screenshot shows the Python Tools for Visual Studio website:

To install Python Tools for Visual Studio, grab the installer from `http://pytools.codeplex.com/` (shown in the preceding screenshot). Also, if you don't own Visual Studio, the Python Tools can be installed on Visual Studio for Desktop or Visual Studio for Web, which are free downloads by Microsoft. You can download the express editions at `http://www.visualstudio.com/products/visual-studio-express-vs`.

 If you intend to use the express editions, I recommend that you download Visual Studio Express for Web, since we will use some HTML and CSS later in the book.

The following screenshot shows the IronPython website:

You might also notice IronPython at `http://ironpython.net/`. IronPython is Python optimized for Windows with access to the .NET libraries, which means that you can access .NET properties with Python, such as `System.Windows.Forms`.

For this book, we will use CPython, (typically referred to as normal Python libraries with nothing added). Keep in mind that some libraries written in Python might or might not work in IronPython, depending on its dependencies.

Let's build a quick Python script in Visual Studio with Python Tools before moving on to OS X. In the following screenshot, you will see the **New Project** window. Notice the options for normal (CPython) called **Python Application** as well as other project types such as **Django** and **IronPython**. We want **Python Application** for this book.

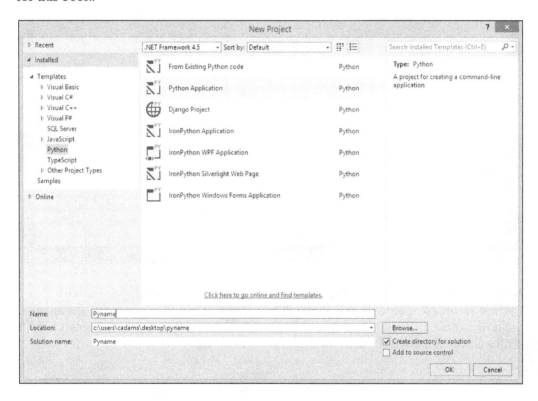

Once you've installed the Python Tools for Visual Studio, open Visual Studio, create a new project under Python, choose **Python Application**, and name it Pyname, as shown in the preceding screenshot. Right-click on the Pyname project and click on **Properties**. Set your interpreter to **Python 2.7** and click on **Save** in the toolbar, as shown in the following screenshot:

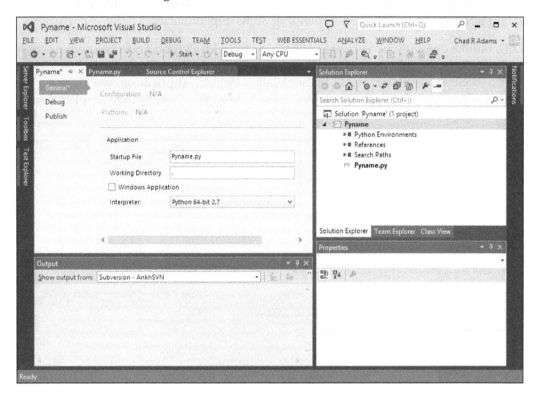

Now, take a look at **Solution Explorer** and expand your **Python Environments | Python 32-bit 2.7**. You'll be able to see that the third-party libraries we've installed are now visible in Visual Studio, as shown in the following screenshot (shown here with a 64-bit version of Python for demo purposes):

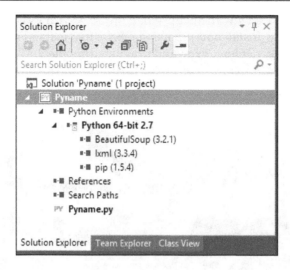

Let's write our `authorName` script that we used earlier, and run it in Visual Studio. Type the following into the `Pyname.py` file:

```
authorName = ('Chad')
print(authorName)
```

Now hit **Start** and you'll see the command prompt automatically launch with `Chad` printed on the screen. Success; you just wrote Python in Visual Studio!

In this section, we covered the following topics:

- Installing Python in Windows
- Installing easy_install and pip
- Installing `lxml`, a common Python library

Setting up Python on Mac OS X

From here on, Python gets easier to install. If you're on a Mac, many consider Python the best to be run on due to the inclusion of build tools and compilers. Before we install Python, it's important to know that OS X includes Python with the OS. One issue, though, is that it doesn't include everything that the base installer does. Also, OS X locks out some command-line features that are common in Unix systems that can cause issues for some Python modules and libraries.

In this section, we will review the Eclipse IDE on OS X with PyDev 3.0 and review using easy_install and pip using OSX. First, install Python by going to `https://www.python.org/` and downloading the 2.7.7 (or higher) 32-bit `.dmg` installer.

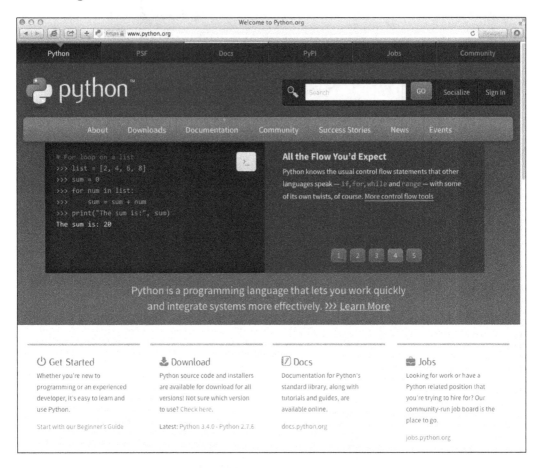

Once it's installed, open the terminal and test easy_install. Since easy_install is included by default, we can use easy_install to install pip. Type the following command in your console:

```
sudo easy_install pip
```

Remember, using `sudo` in the console will prompt you for your administrator password. Depending on your version, your output might mention that you have it already installed; that's okay, this means that your package managers for Python are ready. Now, try testing the Python compiler. In the terminal, type `python` and press the return key.

This should look something like the following screenshot; notice the version number in the interpreter to confirm which version is active.

```
●○○                    ⌂ cadams — Python — 73×23
cadams-new-mac:~ cadams$ sudo easy_install pip
Password:
Searching for pip
Best match: pip 1.3.1
Processing pip-1.3.1-py2.7.egg
pip 1.3.1 is already the active version in easy-install.pth
Installing pip script to /usr/local/bin
Installing pip-2.7 script to /usr/local/bin

Using /Library/Python/2.7/site-packages/pip-1.3.1-py2.7.egg
Processing dependencies for pip
Finished processing dependencies for pip
cadams-new-mac:~ cadams$ python
Python 2.7.6 (v2.7.6:3a1db0d2747e, Nov 10 2013, 00:42:54)
[GCC 4.2.1 (Apple Inc. build 5666) (dot 3)] on darwin
Type "help", "copyright", "credits" or "license" for more information.
>>> █
```

Now, let's test the interpreter; try typing the following command:

```
print('Hello Reader!')
```

The output should be `Hello Reader!`. Now, let's try our `authorName` variable script (shown in the following screenshot) to confirm that variables in Python are being saved. Type both lines shown in the following screenshot, and it should look like the following example. If so, congrats; Python and its base libraries are installed!

```
>>> authorName = 'Chad'
>>> print(authorName)
Chad
>>> █
```

With Python installed, we can now focus on an editor. There are several Python IDEs out for OS X, Aptana, and Pycharm, but the one we will use (and the one that tends to be popular among Python developers) is PyDev for Eclipse. At the time of writing this, Eclipse Kepler (4.3.2) has released, as has PyDev Version 3.0. Both require Java 7 and JDK 7 or higher installed for PyDev to work properly. So, before installing Eclipse and PyDev, install the latest JRE and JDK by visiting the following links:

- http://java.com/en/download/
- http://www.oracle.com/technetwork/java/javase/downloads/index. html

Once you've installed both Java runtime and JDK, reboot your Mac and navigate your browser of choice to http://www.eclipse.org and download the Eclipse Kepler (4.3.2) classic edition (32-bit or 64-bit, depending on your system). The classic edition is Eclipse by itself, with no plugins or project types included. Once this is done, extract the Eclipse .zip file to a folder on your desktop and open the Eclipse application. On launching Eclipse the first time, set your workspace path and click on **OK**. Eclipse will reboot and relaunch Eclipse. Also on Safari, we might get a **Plug-in blocked for this site** message. To continue, the user must click on **Trust**. This is a security measure to confirm that the user wants to install an external package or a plugin. Click on **Trust** to install.

Also, you'll need the JDK and Java 7 runtime or higher, since it's required for the current version of PyDev. The process for the OS X installation should be the same.

Now, with Eclipse loaded, navigate to **Help | Eclipse Marketplace**. Then, in the **Search** field, type Pydev. You should see something like the following screenshot:

Click on **Install Now** and follow the prompts, including approving the certificate by selecting the **I agree** radio button for PyDev and clicking on **Finish**, followed by quitting Eclipse. Once Eclipse is restarted, you can change the IDE for Python development by navigating to **Window | Open Perspective | Other | Pydev** and clicking on **OK**.

Next, let's configure our interpreter so that when we run our Python code, the IDE can process our run requests. The easiest way is in Eclipse.

Navigate to **Window | Preferences | PyDev | Interpreter (Python/Jython/ IronPython)**.

Then, run **Auto Config** by clicking on **Auto Config** in the interpreter window. Your paths will be set up automatically. If you run into an issue, you can set it manually and point to the executable by navigating to **Library | Frameworks | Python. Framework | Versions | 2.7 | bin | python2.7-32**.

Now, let's write some code with Eclipse. With Eclipse restarted, navigate to **File | New | Pydev Project**.

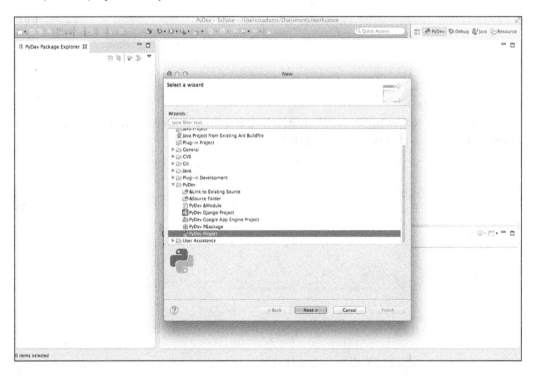

Create a project with the `Pyname` name, as shown in the following screenshot. Next, create a `pyname.py` file in the project explorer on the right.

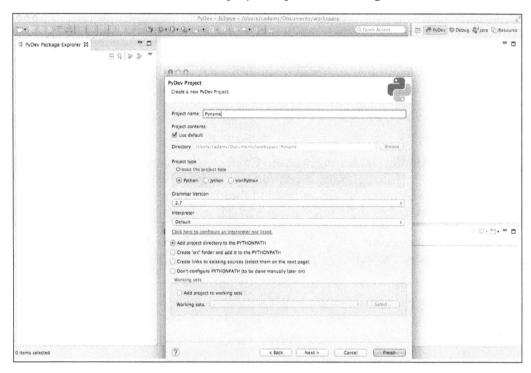

Finally, type the following code as shown in the following screenshot and click on **Run**. If successful, you will see `Chad` in the output window.

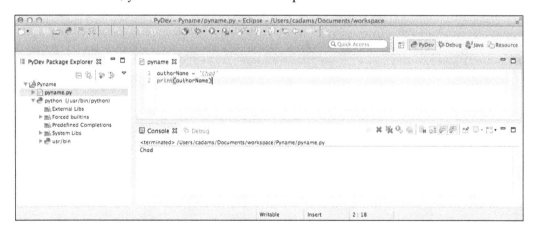

In this section, we covered how to install Python on OS X, installing pip using easy_install, working with the terminal, and setting up Eclipse with PyDev.

Setting up Python on Ubuntu

Linux-based operating systems such as Ubuntu are Python's home in many ways. The Ubuntu marketplace is written in Python, and many Linux apps usually have a Python code base. Ubuntu features many of the same terminal commands OS X uses, if not the same commands. For Ubuntu, we will focus on Ubuntu 13.10. If you're using a derivative of Ubuntu, Lubuntu, Xubuntu, or Linux Mint, there are a few points that need to be kept in mind.

Most of these commands should be the same, with a few minor differences depending on your setup. Reach out to your search engine of choice if you run into issues loading each software component. The same can be said for Debian or Red Hat-based Linux distros.

Like OS X, you'll need the Java 7 runtime or higher and JDK 7 runtime or higher. Ubuntu does not include these in its included package manager, but you can install them via the command line.

The good news is that Python 2.7 is included with Ubuntu 13.10, so we will not need to install Python. We can even test this by opening the terminal and typing `python` in the Bash prompt, as shown in the following screenshot:

```
chad@chad-Parallels-Virtual-Platform: ~
chad@chad-Parallels-Virtual-Platform:~$ python
Python 2.7.5+ (default, Sep 19 2013, 13:48:49)
[GCC 4.8.1] on linux2
Type "help", "copyright", "credits" or "license" for more information.
>>>
```

We will then be taken into the Python interpreter, which will show you the version number of the default Python instance, in this case, 2.7.5+.

The easy_install and pip Python package managers are commonly used to install and update our packages. Next, grab both easy_install and pip, and install both of these tools using the following commands:

```
sudo apt-get install python-setuptools
sudo apt-get install python-pip
```

Remember, in Ubuntu the `sudo` command will ask for a password before installing the `python-setuptools` and `python-pip`. Now, if this is successful, the terminal should return the following message, as shown in the following screenshot:

```
chad@chad-Parallels-Virtual-Platform: ~
chad@chad-Parallels-Virtual-Platform:~$ python
Python 2.7.5+ (default, Feb 27 2014, 19:37:08)
[GCC 4.8.1] on linux2
Type "help", "copyright", "credits" or "license" for more information.
>>> exit(0)
chad@chad-Parallels-Virtual-Platform:~$ sudo apt-get install python-setuptools
[sudo] password for chad:
Reading package lists... Done
Building dependency tree
Reading state information... Done
The following NEW packages will be installed:
  python-setuptools
0 upgraded, 1 newly installed, 0 to remove and 0 not upgraded.
Need to get 455 kB of archives.
After this operation, 1,147 kB of additional disk space will be used.
Get:1 http://us.archive.ubuntu.com/ubuntu/ saucy/main python-setuptools all 0.6.
37-1ubuntu1 [455 kB]
Fetched 455 kB in 0s (537 kB/s)
Selecting previously unselected package python-setuptools.
(Reading database ... 194009 files and directories currently installed.)
Unpacking python-setuptools (from .../python-setuptools_0.6.37-1ubuntu1_all.deb)
...
Setting up python-setuptools (0.6.37-1ubuntu1) ...
chad@chad-Parallels-Virtual-Platform:~$
```

Next, before installing Eclipse with PyDev, let's download Java 7 and JDK. To do this, we will add it to our system package repository and install Java. Open the terminal and type the following commands:

```
sudo add-apt-repository ppa:webupd8team/java
sudo apt-get update
sudo apt-get install oracle-java7-installer
```

Be sure to use the keyboard keys on the licensing agreement in the terminal, as shown in the following screenshot:

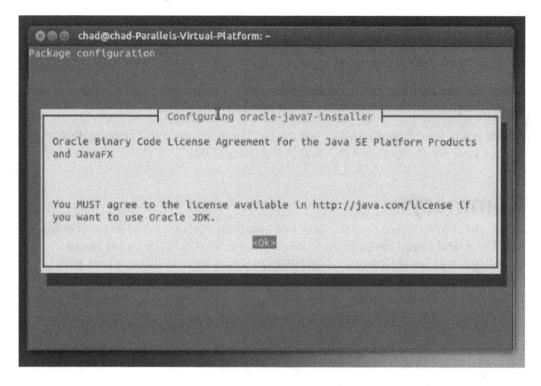

When this is complete, you can test the installation by typing `Java -version` in the terminal. This command will return the installed version of Java.

Now, let's install Eclipse and PyDev. Navigate to `http://www.eclipse.org/` using your browser of choice, and download Eclipse Classic. Unpack the download and open Eclipse, then select a workspace path, and click on **OK**.

At the time of writing this, there is a bug for Eclipse's menus being reskinned in Ubuntu. If you're experiencing this issue, check online for a command-line fix, as this can vary between updates. Ubuntu 14.04 LTS is planned in order to have this bug resolved in the release.

Once this is done, open **Eclipse Marketplace** by navigating to **Help | Eclipse Marketplace** and search for PyDev. Install the plugin and agree to the certificate, then reboot Eclipse.

Assuming everything is installed properly, you'll see PyDev in the **Preferences** section of Eclipse.

One final note on Ubuntu: since Ubuntu has its own package manager, `apt-get`, we can install packages for Python using it as well, for example, using `lxml`:

```
sudo apt-get install python-lxml
```

Notice that we add a `python-` prefix before our package. This helps `apt-get` specify package types, since `apt-get` works with multiple languages.

At this point, you should be all set for the Python development. Try recreating our `authorName` script from our OS X and Windows sections.

Summary

In this chapter, we went over the basics of installing Python and tools for Windows, Mac OS X, and Linux-based Python development. Next, with our tools ready, we will go over some Python coding basics to warm up to building charts with Python code.

2
Python Refresher

In this chapter, we'll go over some Python programming basics and common Python first- and third-party libraries used in Python development. In this chapter, we'll be working on Python Tools for Visual Studio, which works well for new Python developers, using standard 2.7 CPython. It will be fine if you're working on Mac, Linux Eclipse, or an editor of your choice. We will be using pip and easy_install in Visual Studio, but I will include notes for Mac and Linux commands as well.

Python basics

Let's start with creating a project in Visual Studio with Python Tools (VSPT). Go to **File** | **New Project**, then **Python** | **Python Application**, and call this solution Chapter2, as shown in the following screenshot:

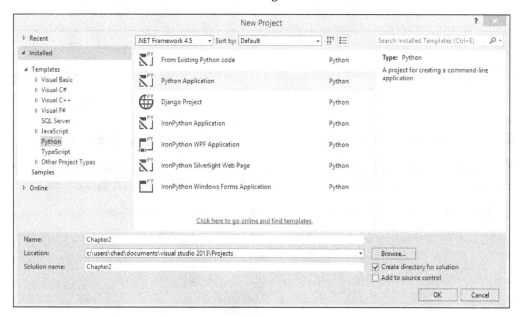

Next, navigate to **Solution Explorer** and click on **Add/Remove Environments**. You'll see the prompt as shown in the following screenshot. If you have multiple Python installs, you'll be able to select which one you want to specify. Click on the **Python 2.7** environment and click on **OK**.

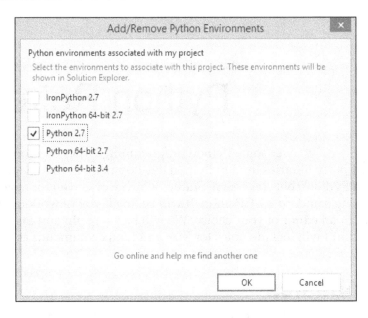

So what does this do? A common problem with Python development is that libraries installed on your host system using pip or easy_install are kept outside your project files. This makes using Python scripts with different libraries installed on one system unable to run on another system without the exact same setup. It will also update Visual Studio's IntelliSense for any Python libraries installed as best as it can.

Now look at your **Solution Explorer**. You'll see that **Python 2.7** has been added under **Python Environments**. You can see where the copied environment is saved in your project by right-clicking on **Python 2.7** and clicking on **Open Folder in File Explorer**. You'll see a `Lib` folder with a subfolder called `site-packages` that has been created with its own lib structure for third-party modules and libraries.

Now let's write some code by starting with the canonical Hello World application for Python. Type in the following code in your editor and click on **Start** at the top:

```
print("Hello, World") #This will execute the quickest and fastest, but
doesn't scale well in Python.
```

Many small Python scripts are written this way with no structure or containment. This can be an issue as your application gets bigger. Let's wrap this in a function. Type the following code in your editor again, and click on **Start** at the top:

```
#A simple python function.
def main():
    print("Hello, World")


main() #Called after main() is loaded into memory.
```

Here, we have created a function called `main()` and included our `print` statement inside it. On the next line, we called `main()` to trigger the console to print `Hello World`. If you're coming from a C# or JavaScript background, this may look a little funny, and you're right to think so. Python is a very loose language — there are no braces wrapping the function and no semicolons to terminate a line of code.

This keeps typing to a minimum, which is great, but for those who have never coded Python before, this can cause issues. Python is very specific on how its code is structured in order for it to work. Remember that at the start of the book, errors like these can trip up development. Let's look at an example:

```
#A simple python function.
def main():
    print("Hello, World") '''A function needs to be indented and not
be further away more than one line break.'''
main()
```

By using an IDE like Visual Studio or Eclipse, we can see issues like these, whereas a simple text editor might not show these issues. The following is Visual Studio showing an indent issue. Move the mouse over the `print()` method and you'll get help on what the issue is.

So far, this is working well for a small Python script, but let's start moving our code to a more object-oriented structure. Now, we want to wrap our `main()` function and have it trigger with one of our Python built-in script events, specifically, our `__main__` event. Note the double underscores, which indicate that it's a built-in event in Python. Here's an example of the `__main__` event being triggered on the `main()` function:

```
#Same function as before.
def main():
    print("Hello, World")
if __name__ == '__main__': #Here Python checks if the runtime event
__main__ is called if so run the code below.
    main()
```

You can see that we check the `__name__` event for `__main__`; if it is present, the function or functions are executed. This is similar to a `private void` function in C# or `window.onload` in JavaScript. It's also important to wrap functions this way should you want to create your own Python module library, so that each can be called only when the module is fully loaded and not before.

Now, let's add a parameter so we can reuse our `main()` function. Here, I'll add the username to the `main()` function so I can pass a string to our `Hello` print statement:

```
#Main function with passed in parameter.
def main(readersname):
    print("Hello, " + readersname)


if __name__ == '__main__':
    main('Chad')
```

Note that you can append strings using + just as when using JavaScript or C#. You also have the option of string formatters in Python. Here's the preceding code with a string formatter passing in our `readersname` parameter:

```
#Here we use string formatting to better construct our strings.
def main(readersname):
    print("Hello, %s" % readersname)


if __name__ == '__main__':
    main('Chad')
```

Let's add another parameter to our `main()` method. This time, we will use a number, specifically an integer. Let's pass the number 35 as a set number of pages the reader has read and update our `print()` statement to include both:

```
#Main function with two passed in parameters.
def main(readersname, amt):
    print("Hello, " + readersname + ", you have read " + str(amt) + "
pages.")


if __name__ == '__main__':
    main('Chad', 35)
```

Run the script and the output will be `Hello, Chad, you have read 35 pages..` Next, let's use string formatting here rather than using string concatenation. I've changed the string concatenation to a string formatter using `%i` to indicate that the format is an integer:

```
#Here we use string formatting to better construct our strings.
def main(readersname, amt):
    print("Hello, %s, you have read %i" % (readersname, amt))


if __name__ == '__main__':
    main('Chad', 35)
```

String formatting can also help parameters output in unique ways. Let's say we wanted to show 35 as a float with decimal points. We can change our string integer formatter `%i` to a float formatter, `%f`. Look at this example:

```
#Let's format the string to output a float with decimal places.
def main(readersname, amt):
    print("Hello, %s, your total pages read are %f." % (readersname,
amt))


if __name__ == '__main__':
    main('Chad', 50)
```

If we run the Python script, you'll see the output `Hello, Chad, your total pages read are 50.000000.`. As we can see, the integer value we passed is now `50.000000` with our float formatter modifying our string without any conversion code. Now what if we wanted this to display only two decimal points? Well, we can tweak our modifier and specify how many decimal points as shown in the following code:

```
#Let's format the string to output a float with two decimal places.
def main(readersname, amt):
    print("Hello, %s, your total pages read are %0.2f." %
(readersname, amt))

if __name__ == '__main__':
    main('Chad', 50)
```

If we run the Python script now our output looks like this: `Hello, Chad, your total pages read are 50.00.`

Formatters work on floats to integers as well; look at this code sample:

```
def main(readersname, amt):
    print("Hello, %s, your total pages read are %i." % (readersname,
amt))

if __name__ == '__main__':
    main('Chad', 50.652)
```

Now, let's look at our result: `Hello, Chad, your total pages read are 50..` We notice that it removed the decimal places and even though the `.652` value should round our 50 integer to 51, it didn't. The integer formatter simply trimmed the value and didn't round up the value. This is very important to keep in mind for integer formatters.

This is great. Now we have a quick and easy way to convert values to floats (decimal points) and back to integers again should we need to convert values in our charts later on. Remember that Python is a dynamically-typed language, meaning that all variables can be any type without specification, and the Python interpreter assigns a type based on what's available. Now that we have a handle on functions and strings, let's take a look at some common libraries to help us understand file inputs and outputs.

Importing modules and libraries

What we've covered so far could work for very small Python scripts, but we want to use premade libraries and functions to take full advantage of Python to allow us to write maintainable code. In this section, we'll review importing existing Python modules and libraries and using those functions in our code.

Recall that in *Chapter 1, Setting Up Your Development Environment*, we covered installing pip and easy_install. Well, pip at least is a Python library, but one thing you may not recollect is that in that chapter, we in fact installed many libraries and modules. If you recall, we also installed the Python language interpreter and tools from `https://www.python.org/`. Our install came with hundreds of bundled libraries to be used. These are considered the general release libraries for Python. These are common language libraries used in Python development and tested by the Python Software Foundation for cross-platform development, which removes the need for OS-specific development in the core language.

Let's try importing the `sys` module. The `sys` module provides access to some variables used or maintained by the interpreter and to functions that interact strongly with the interpreter.

To import a module, type in the following on the topmost line of your Python script.

```
import sys
```

Have a look at this step in the following screenshot:

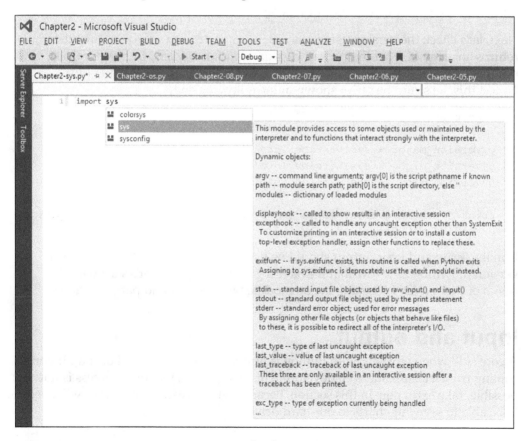

In Visual Studio, you can call up IntelliSense while you type by pressing *Ctrl* + Space bar. You can see IntelliSense filter more and more as you type. Also, whatever is highlighted will show Python docstrings that are written for that file to provide help and notes to the developer implementing those libraries.

If you're in Eclipse, the Eclipse PyDev also provides code hinting, just like IntelliSense. Even the keyboard shortcut is the same, *Ctrl* + Spacebar. Now let's test our import. Since `sys` can look up Python arguments and environment variables, let's check what platform we're running. Type in the following in your editor:

```
import sys

platform = sys.platform;

print("%s" % platform)
```

Now run the script and if you're in a Windows-based OS, your output would be `win32`; if you're on Mac OS X, your output would be `darwin` (this is referring to the FreeBSD Apple implementation of FreeBSD, which is the core of OS X). If you're on a Linux OS like Ubuntu, your output will be `linux2`.

Next, let's check the version using `sys.version_info`. The `version_info` list returns an array of what the current version used for this script, a major release number (int), a minor release number (int), and a micro release number (int). To test this, let's run the script shown in the following code:

```
import sys

pyversion_major = sys.version_info[0];
pyversion_minor = sys.version_info[1];
pyversion_micro = sys.version_info[2];

print("Python version: %s.%s.%s" % (pyversion_major, pyversion_minor, pyversion_micro))
```

Run the script and your output should be `Python version: 2.7.6` or a newer version of Python 2.7. Now that we have a grasp on imports, let's start with the basics of Python file I/O using the `os` module with its user and path functions.

Input and output

A core skill when working with Python is understanding input and output. If you're coming from a client-side web development background, where file access is not possible, take extra note in this section, because when creating charts, we will need to be able to save our charts to our hard drive.

The `os` module is one of the most used modules in Python mostly because of how it handles getting common filepaths cross-platform. Let's demonstrate how we can read files. Create a text file called `PyREADME.txt` and save it to your project's directory. Copy the following text in the `PyREADME.txt` file and save the file:

```
Hello Reader,
This copy is being read in Python, and saved as a string to a
variable.
```

Once saved, it should look like the following screenshot:

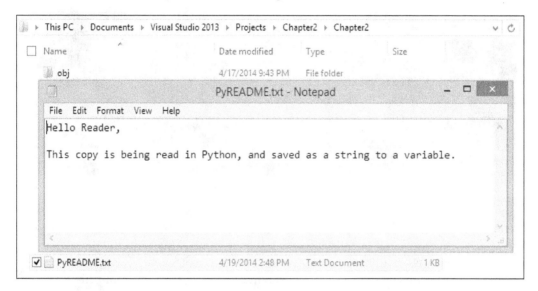

Now, in your Python editor, we will import the `os` module by including `import os` on the topmost line and then add the following code. Be sure your `PyREADME.txt` file is in the same directory as your running Python script.

```python
import os

#Open the file to be read.
openFile = os.open('PyREADME.txt', os.O_RDONLY )

#Save the file's inner content to a Python variable string. This take
two parameters, the file to be opened and how many characters to read.
readmeText = os.read(openFile, 100)

print(readmeText)
```

If everything is successful, your output window should show what's in the next figure.

 If you are having issues, double-check your file type and see if you have file extensions such as PyREADME.txt.

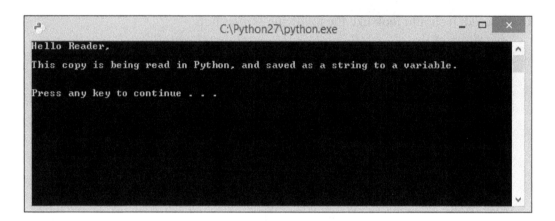

Now let's review our code. We open our file using the open() function, and we have two parameters: our file name with an extension and an r string. The r string tells the open() method what permissions we have when working with the file. After we open the file, we read the file and print it to the console. Lastly, we close our openFile; this keeps us from having a potential memory leak, since our file I/O won't close until we tell it to close.

Next, let's create a text file. We will have Hello World as its content, and name it content.txt. Replace your Python file with this bit of code:

```
import os

txtContent = 'Hello World'
openFile = open('content.txt', 'w') #Open the file to be written.
readmeText = openFile.write(txtContent) #Write the file's inner
content to the text file.

openFile.close() #Close the file.
```

If successful, you should have a new text file with `Hello World` written in the file, as shown in the next screenshot. You can find the file in the same directory as your Python script. Let's review the code. You'll notice that we changed our `open()` permission's parameter to `w`, which means write-only, and we've set the filename to `content.txt` to indicate the name of the file (even if it doesn't exist prior to running the script). Beyond that, the only code that's changed is because we've swapped `openFile.read()` with `openFile.write()`, telling Python to write a content string to the file rather than the output from a file.

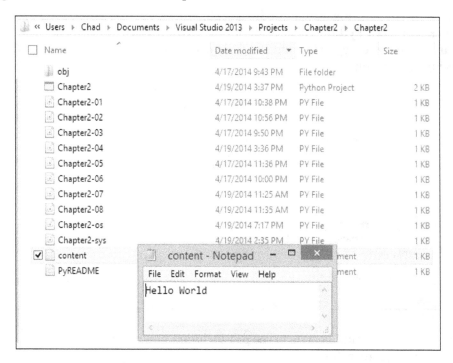

Generating an image

Now that we understand imports and reading and writing a file to the hard drive of our computer, let's generate an image with some text. The first thing to be done is downloading an imaging library to use since Python doesn't include one by default. The most common of these is the **Python Imaging Library** (**PIL**). PIL allows text input to be printed as an image and is very commonly used for CAPTCHA password systems.

To install PIL, we will need to use easy_install. If you have Mac OS X or Linux, the command is as follows:

```
sudo easy_install PIL
```

On Windows, you can run the following in the command line as the administrator in the Python directory:

```
easy_install PIL
```

Better yet, if you're using Visual Studio as your editor, set your project to **Python 2.7** and click on **Install Python Package** under the **Python Environments 2.7** instance. Type in `pil` under easy_install and check **Run as Administrator** as shown in the following screenshot:

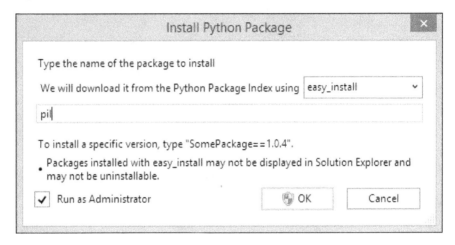

If successful, you should be able to see `pil` included in your environments, as shown in the following screenshot:

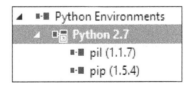

In other environments such as Eclipse, you can check your import by using the following command:

```
from pil import *
```

This will import all modules from the PIL library. Now that we have that set, we are going to reuse the content.txt file we created earlier and generate an image with its content. Since this is a bit more complicated, I'll move both steps into their own functions, as shown in the following code:

```python
from pil import *
import Image
import ImageDraw
import os

def readcontent():
    '''Open the file to be read. Note the file's permission is set to
read-only.'''
    openFile = open('content.txt', 'r')
    '''Save the file's inner content to a Python Variable string.'''
    readmeText = openFile.read()
    '''Close the file to save memory.'''
    openFile.close()
    '''Return the results to each as a reference variable.'''
    return openFile, readmeText


def generateImage():
    '''Create our references.'''
    img = Image.new("RGBA", (100, 80), "white")
    '''Draw the images size and background to the screen.'''
    draw = ImageDraw.Draw(img)
    '''Position the text with an x/y of 10 x 10, assign it the text
value and text color of red.'''
    output = draw.text((10, 10), readmeText,  fill=(255,0,0,255))
    '''Draw the text to the screen.'''
    draw = ImageDraw.Draw(img)
    '''Save the image.'''
    img.save("output.png")
    '''Return the results to each as a reference variable.'''
    return draw, img, output

'''trigger the read content function.'''
openFile, readmeText = readcontent()

'''Generate our image.'''
draw, img, output = generateImage()
```

We should now have a simple image like the one shown in the following screenshot. Feel free to modify the content.txt file for different results if you want to set the font size and font.

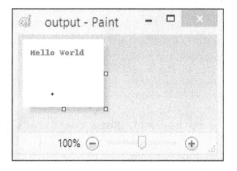

There is a bug in the current version of PIL through easy_install. Some of the C-based code doesn't install properly. You may want to check out pillow (a bundled version of PIL), which you can download here: https://code.google.com/p/rudix/downloads/detail?name=pillow-1.7.7-0.pkg&can=2&q.

Creating SVG graphics using svgwrite

Before we close this chapter, let's take a look at how to generate SVG graphics that are based on vectors and computer-drawn lines and shapes that are scalable. To do this, we are going to use a Python library called svgwrite, which you can find here: https://pypi.python.org/pypi/svgwrite. Since this is a Python library on PyPi, we can use pip to install it.

For Windows users using VSPT

Add your current Python instance to your Python environments in your **Solution Explorer** and type in svgwrite in the **Install Python Package** prompt as shown in the following screenshot:

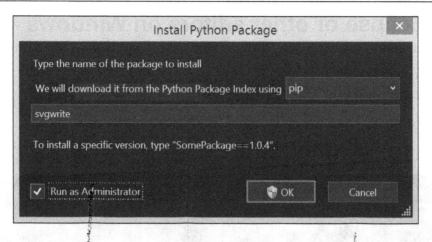

If successful, you should see the packages in your **Solution Explorer** as shown in the following screenshot. If you can't see them, try opening your **Python Environments**, and then your version of Python in your solution:

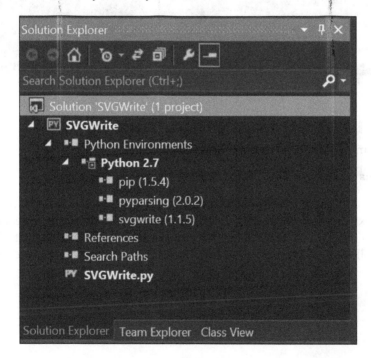

For Eclipse or other editors on Windows

Type in the following command in your command prompt with admin rights:

```
cd C:\Python27
```

```
pip install svgwrite
```

The following is a screenshot of a command prompt for Windows:

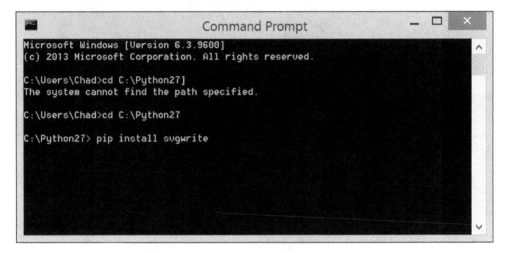

For Eclipse on Mac and Linux

Open the terminal and type in the following command:

```
sudo pip install svgwrite
```

We are using `sudo` here to ensure everything for `svgwrite` has been installed properly. Next, create your project in PyDev and be sure to set the project path to `src`. This sets the path to its own directory rather than your Python root. Have a look at the following screenshot showing the start of a new PyDev project in Eclipse on OS X:

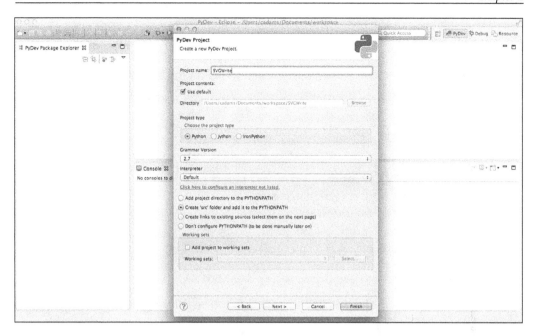

In Eclipse, you can also inspect code using the Python console. In your console, click on the **New Console View** icon at the top-right of the window and select **Pydev Console** as shown in the following screenshot:

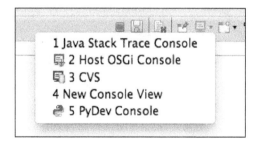

You can also verify in PyDev what packages you have installed. In your **PyDev Package Explorer**, expand the **python** root and go to **System Libs | 2.7/site-packages**. Once open, if you can find svgwrite, you should be set. In the following screenshot, you can see how it looks on my system:

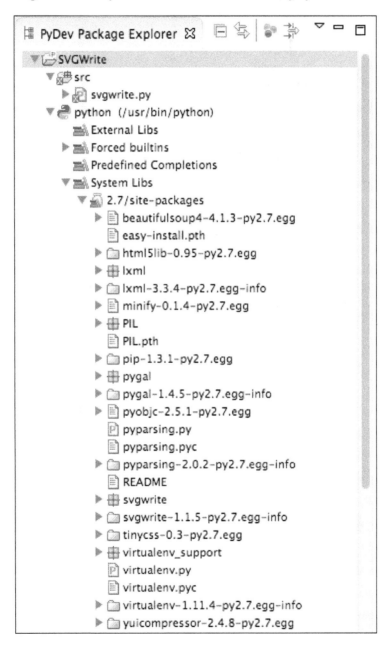

Once you're ready, we will create a new project and Python file to generate our SVG file. Start by creating an import of `svgwrite` (in lowercase) as shown in the following code:

```
import svgwrite
```

Now let's reference the root `svgwrite` library and assign it to a variable that we can output as an SVG file. For this, we will use the `Drawing` method in `svgwrite`. The `Drawing` method enables us to create an SVG file. It's where we will drop our other objects such as text, lines, circles, and so on.

Let's take a look at the following example:

```
drawObj = svgwrite.Drawing('username.svg', profile='tiny', width=444,
height=300)
```

Here, we have a `drawObj` variable and we have created an instance of the `svgwrite` object and called the `Drawing` method with a few parameters. Our first parameter is a string where we declare our filename; in this case, `username.svg`. Note that we are not including a path, so for this script, the file will be saved in our project directory.

The `profile` attribute sets the base profile for SVG. You have two values that you can use: `tiny` and `full`. We can also set the width and height of the SVG tag with the `width` and `height` attributes.

Now, we have the base drawing object to draw shapes on. We will append the `drawObj` variable with an SVG text node. Take a look at the following line:

```
drawObj.add(drawObj.text('Test', insert=(0, 0), fill='red', font_
size=70, font_family='sans-serif', font_weight='bold'))
```

So here we have a series of parameters for our line. The first is a string for the text copy we want to write into the node and the next is a map (a map is a group of two parameters). This map sets the X and Y coordinates for our top-left text block element in the SVG node.

Following that is our `fill` color for this text block; in this case, we have a value of `red`. We can also use hex values here if we need it to be similar to a color hex in CSS. We also have three more parameters here: `font_size`, `font_family`, and `font_weight`, all of which are pretty self-explanatory. The `font_size` parameter uses simple int values to increase or decrease size. The `font_family` parameter will work with any regular font included on the system (no file path needed). And `font_weight` can set the font's weight to be `bold` or `light` depending on the selected font's properties. Take note, without the `font_family` parameter, the `font_weight` parameter will not work.

Lastly, we will save the `drawObj` variable to a file using the `save()` function. This will save the file with the parameters we added. With that added, here's a completed script ready to run. Here's our `save()` function:

```
drawObj.save()
```

Now let's run the application from our IDE. Check your code as you follow along with the `drawObj` sample shown in the previous code, and assuming no errors are encountered, you should see a terminal (or a command prompt) window with **Press Enter to continue...** displayed just like the previous example, indicating success.

We can check this by going into our project directory and opening our newly generated `username.svg` file in our browser of choice and taking a look:

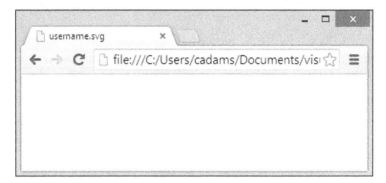

We're almost there. It looks like our SVG file is fine, but our text node is off-center. Remember our `insert` map, where we defined our X and Y coordinates? Let's tweak that; also, if you are working on Ubuntu or any other Linux distro, you may need to format the X and Y coordinates to fit your platform's browser:

```
drawObj.add(drawObj.text('Test', insert=(15, 64), fill='red', font_
size=70, font_family='sans-serif', font_weight='bold'))
```

Let's rerun and refresh our SVG file in our browser:

There is our text, showing up as an SVG we generated. Note that we can even select the text. Since this is a text node, we should be able to highlight and even search it inside the web content. Having the output as SVG gives us a range of uses to create graphics.

Let's add a few lines around our text node, like an X and Y chart baseline, just to show some basic drawing. Before your `save()` function, include the `line()` functions as shown in in the following example:

```
import svgwrite

drawObj = svgwrite.Drawing('username.svg', profile='tiny', width=444,
height=300)
drawObj.add(drawObj.text('Test', insert=(15, 64), fill='red', font_
size=70, font_family='sans-serif', font_weight='bold'))
drawObj.add(drawObj.line((10, 10), (10, 70), stroke=svgwrite.rgb(0, 0,
0, '%')))
drawObj.add(drawObj.line((10, 70), (370, 70), stroke=svgwrite.rgb(0,
0, 0, '%')))
drawObj.save()
```

Now let's rerun our project and take a look at the results:

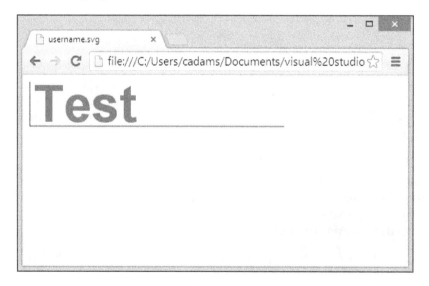

Now we have the start of what would be a very simple chart exported as an SVG file that we can manipulate in HTML (using an SVG-compliant browser). Take a look at the following screenshot. Here, we can change the `fill` color using Chrome's Web Inspector:

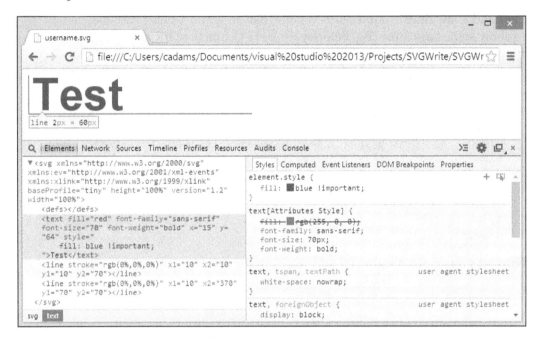

Neat! So now we can print text and objects to an SVG file! We can draw lines, boxes, and circles in SVG, and as you see this come along, you start to get an idea how to build charts and graphs from scratch. Let's make this script a bit more functional, as though we were using this as an application. Let's reuse our text file reader module from our Hello World image script.

Before starting with this code, ensure your `content.txt` file is at the root of your project directory. Next, let's reuse our `readcontent()` function from our earlier script. Breaking up that code in a module early on helps us reuse the code in new projects by copying and pasting!

Firstly, include your imports, which will contain `svgwrite`, just like before to access your text file:

```
import svgwrite

def readcontent():
    '''Open the file to be read. Note the file's permission is set to
    read-only.'''
```

```
    openFile = open('content.txt', 'r')
    '''Save the file's inner content to a Python Variable string.'''
    readmeText = openFile.read()
    '''Close the file to save memory.'''
    openFile.close()
    '''Return the results to each as a reference variable.'''
    return openFile, readmeText

'''trigger the read content function.'''
openFile, readmeText = readcontent()
```

Now let's wrap our `svgwrite` in its own function and give it a parameter; in this case, `username`, to pass our `content.txt` file's output. Your Python script should resemble the following code:

```
import svgwrite
def readcontent():
    '''Open the file to be read. Note the file's permission is set
to read-only.'''
    openFile = open('content.txt', 'r')

    readmeText = openFile.read()
    '''Save the file's inner content to a Python Variable string.'''

    openFile.close()
    '''Close the file to save memory.'''

    return openFile, readmeText
    '''Return the results to each as a reference variable.'''


def createSVGText(usrname):
    drawObj = svgwrite.Drawing('username.svg', profile='tiny',
width=444, height=300)
    drawObj.add(drawObj.text(usrname, insert=(15, 64), fill='red',
font_size=70, font_family='sans-serif', font_weight='bold'))
    drawObj.add(drawObj.line((10, 10), (10, 70), stroke=svgwrite.
rgb(0, 0, 0, '%')))
    drawObj.add(drawObj.line((10, 70), (400, 70), stroke=svgwrite.
rgb(0, 0, 0, '%')))
    drawObj.save()
    return drawObj

'''trigger the read content function.'''
```

```
openFile, readmeText = readcontent()
'''Grab the 'readmeText' file content and pass that into our
createSVGText function.'''
drawObj = createSVGText(readmeText)
```

Rerun the script and let's take a look at our `username.svg` file:

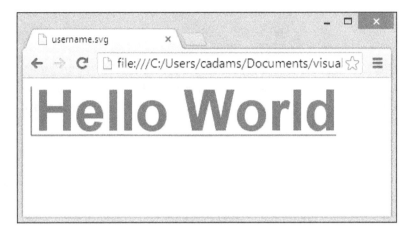

There we are! We have created a dynamic script that pulls in data from a local text file and imports it into a chart-like layout and updates dynamically for each run. Play around with the options and see what you can make, and type other words into the `content.txt` file.

Now this is still a simple script; obviously, if we type in a very long string in our text file, it will overflow the SVG file. This is just one element. What if you were building a chart from scratch and needed everything to work properly? We can assume this will only get more and more complex, and ultimately that is the point of this chapter.

Summary

To wrap up, in this chapter, we reviewed some basic Python skills, variables, functions, and parameters; saw how to import libraries and how to install libraries on multiple IDEs; and generated PNG graphics using the Python Imaging Library, a common Python library.

We took a moment to understand paths and file I/O in Python, reading and writing to files and variables in our Python code. We also learned about SVG graphics: how to work with them and generate them in Python using the `svgwrite` library.

Now that we have done some basic generation of graphics with Python and worked with some basic imaging libraries, we are ready to start the data visualization part of this book.

As you now know, building graphics, let alone charts, can be a monumental task to perform without some helper libraries. Fortunately, Python provides library after library of tested and great-looking charting tools that are ready for your Python projects.

In the next chapter, we will start with a very easy-to-use, almost turnkey library for building SVG charts that is ready with high-end multimedia content: pygal!

3
Getting Started with pygal

In this chapter, we will start with building some basic SVG charts using the **pygal** charting library for Python and look at common chart types and styles.

Why use pygal?

In the world of Python development, there are many libraries for charts (Matplotlib and Plotly being a few examples), and cookbook-style books have been written for many of them. Since this is an introduction to data charting, we need a simple, easy-to-use library where developers new to Python charting, or Python charting in general, could easily take code from this book and build Python applications. The following screenshot shows the pygal website with some chart examples:

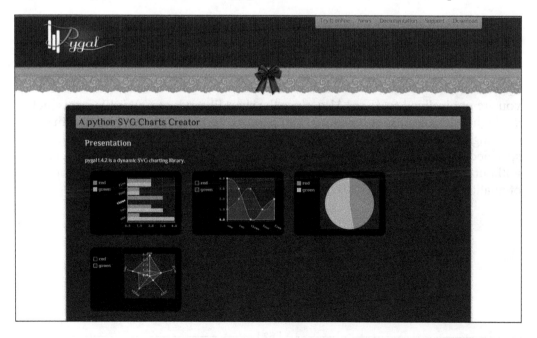

This is where pygal comes in; pygal (`http://pygal.org/`) is a Python-based SVG Charts Creator, developed by the Kozea Community (`http://community.kozea.fr/`), as shown in the following screenshot. This is a group dedicated to building quality open source libraries (mainly Python based, but for HTML5 projects as well).

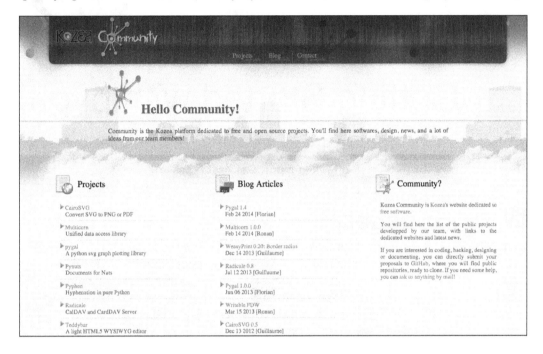

The `pygal` library offers multiple charting options beyond what I consider standard charts: bar charts, line charts, and pie graphs. It includes a world map, funnel charts, radar charts, and box plots, to name just a few.

It also includes prebuilt themes and styles, which you do not have to customize if you are not inclined to do so. Also, since the chart library's output is SVG, this makes it a highly flexible output type for HTML5 or even print media. One issue with some charting libraries in Python is that the output defaults to the PNG format with a specified image size. Since SVG is a vector graphic (a type of graphic that is scalable without losing image quality), it can be scaled and resized for any need without loss of quality.

Take a look at the following screenshot of the documentation page for
`http://pygal.org/`:

The pygal website also includes pretty good and easy-to-read documentation.
One thing that's quite common with third-party Python libraries is that the
documentation can range from a well-documented, online-searchable wiki to a
simple `readme.txt` file that only shows how to install the library. The `pygal` library
also doesn't require a lot of dependencies, which is crucial for an introductory book,
as a very dependent library might cause issues for new developers or developers
who are new to pygal.

Many Python frameworks have some very picky dependencies that you might need for your project, but they might or might not work with your system.

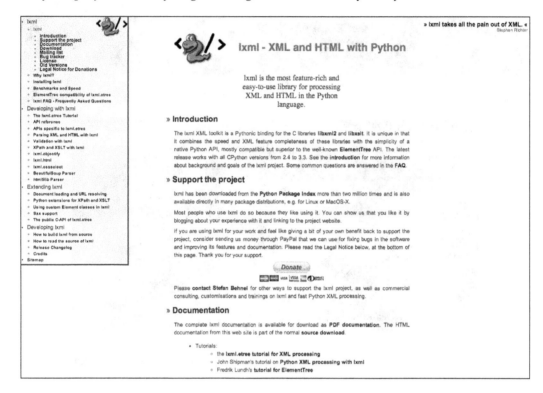

The `lxml` library is the only library required for pygal, but it has a few issues depending on which operating system you are running your Python code on. I encourage you to reread the notes on `lxml` (specifically if you're running Windows) before we cover the installation of pygal.

With that covered, let's install pygal and build some charts!

Installing pygal using pip

First and foremost, if you haven't installed `lxml`, if you're working on Windows, you'll want to install the `lxml` installer, as mentioned in *Chapter 1*, *Setting Up Your Development Environment*; otherwise, the following commands should install `lxml` for you. Next, we will use pip and install `pygal` using the following commands for Windows and Mac/Linux systems (note that `sudo` is used in the Mac and Ubuntu install).

If you are a Windows user, type the following command:

```
pip install pygal
```

If you are a Mac or Ubuntu user, type the following command:

```
sudo pip install pygal
```

Next, open Eclipse with PyDev and create a new Python project, followed by a new file (the settings aren't important since this is a test project). Once the project is created, create the new file, call it importtest.py, and type the following:

```
import pygal
```

If successful, you should be able to press *Ctrl* + Space bar and see PyDev's code hinting pull all of the libraries installed on the system. In the following screenshot, you can see pygal being recognized in my system:

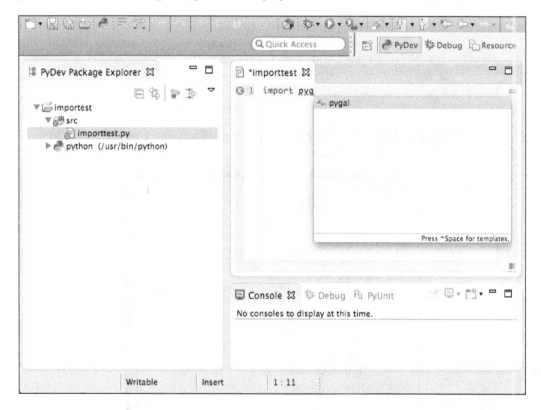

Installing pygal using Python Tools for Visual Studio

If you plan on working in Visual Studio for the remainder of the book, here's a note on installation: first, if you haven't already installed lxml, as noted in *Chapter 1, Setting Up Your Development Environment*, then run **easy_install** with your Python environment in the **Install Python Package** window, as shown in the following screenshot:

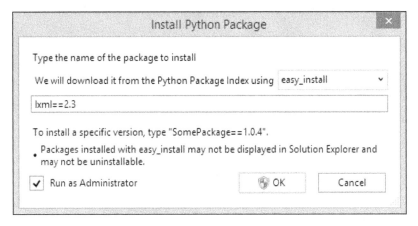

If successful, your **Solution Explorer** window should look like what is shown in the following screenshot with lxml included:

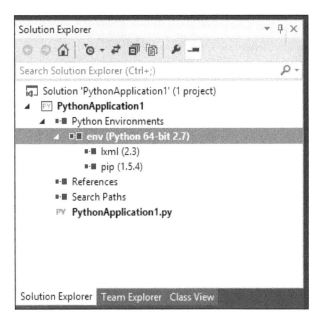

Lastly, install the `pygal` library. Right-click on your environments and select **Install Python Package**, this time with `pygal`, as shown in the following screenshot:

Building a line chart

Line charts typically show how particular data changes at different intervals of time. In charting, this is the simplest chart that you can make, typically with the x and y axes and each axis on the chart indicating time, value, or another parameter.

Let's build a simple chart, in this case, on how many hits a website has received in the past two years (2012–2014). Take a look at the first line in the following code; this is a declarative line by the Python interpreter to specify the type of string encoding to the file. Also, you'll notice on `line.x_labels` that we use an inline function called `range()`. This lets us create an array of numbers, starting from the lowest number to the highest number; in the following case, 2012 and 2014 would print as 2012, 2013, 2014 in an array. Now, copy the following code into your project's main Python file:

```
# -*- coding: utf-8 -*-
import pygal

#create a new line chart.
line = pygal.Line()
line.title = 'Website hits in the past 2 years' #set chart title
line.x_labels = map(str, range(2012, 2014)) #set the x-axis labels.
line.add('Page views', [None, 0, 12, 32, 72, 148]) #set values.
line.render_to_file('linechart.svg') #set filename.
```

The following screenshot shows a basic pygal line chart output:

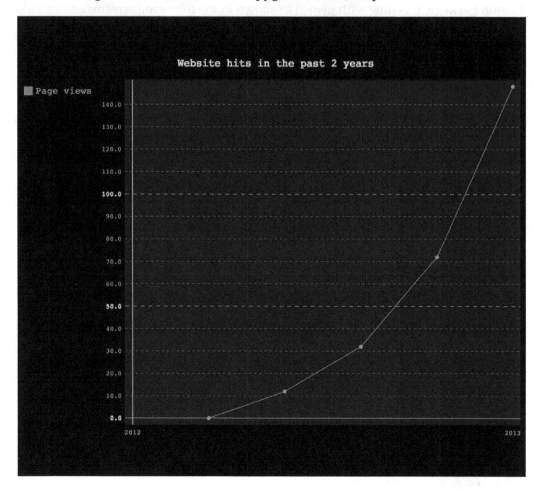

In your main project file where you ran your script, you can see the `linechart.svg` file created. Open it, and your chart will look like what's shown in the preceding screenshot. To find the file, open the directory your project is in and find the `linechart.svg` file. Note that you can hover over the dots and get the values of each marker in the chart; these are some of the functionalities that come prebuilt with the `pygal` library.

We will also see that the chart's timeline starts from 0.0 on 2013. If you take a look at the line.add() statement, the first parameter is None; this adds a spacer in our chart to push the chart data out a little bit rather than forcing the chart to start at 2012. This is a common trick to setting up chart layouts.

Another feature is that if you hover over the line label (in this case, Page views) the entire line will be highlighted, indicating which dataset you're viewing with that label. The pygal library will also review your data and emphasize certain lines on the data axis, such as 0.0, 50.0, and 100.0, to break up some of the chart lines for easier readability.

Code hinting support for the appearance of the line() function for pygal depends on the IDE you are using. The pygal library is written in a slightly unusual way when compared to most Python libraries. The library generates each chart type dynamically using a for loop, which checks each chart class in the pygal library. Due to this, IDEs that require static, hardcoded functions in Python will throw an error, but not break when they are run. In other words, using code hinting might or might not work well depending on the editor you're using.

Stacked line charts

Stacked line charts work in a manner similar to traditional line charts, but they stack multiple sets of data over each other to show the specific values for a group. Copy the following code into your project's main Python file and run the file. Also, take note of the multiple add() functions on our chart. Since the chart has multiple datasets in one chart, we need to create a dataset for each:

```python
# -*- coding: utf-8 -*-
import pygal

#create a new stacked line chart.
line = pygal.StackedLine(fill=True)
line.title = 'Web hits in the past 2 years' #set chart title
line.x_labels = map(str, range(2012, 2014)) #set the x-axis labels.
line.add('Site A', [None, 0, 12, 32, 72, 148]) #set values.
line.add('Site B', [2, 16, 12, 87, 91, 342]) #set values.
line.add('Site C', [42, 55, 84, 88, 90, 171]) #set values.
line.render_to_file('linechart.svg') #set filename.
```

The following screenshot shows the results of our script:

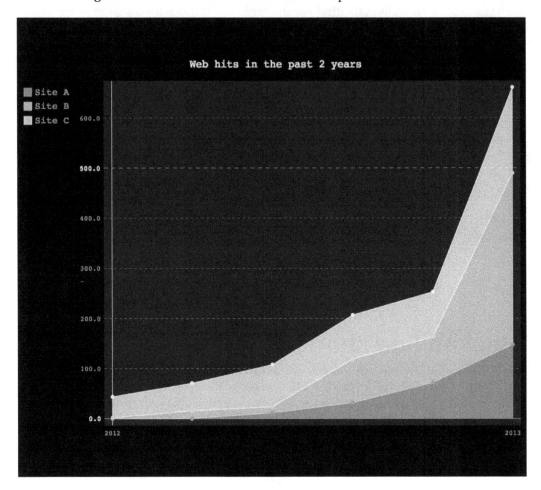

Once rendered, your stacked chart will look like what's shown in the preceding screenshot. Open the directory your project is in to find the `linechart.svg` file. Note how pygal overrides your original SVG file by default; keep this in mind when working with this library. Also, you will notice that we added a `fill=True` parameter to our `StackedLine` function when we declared our chart; this is a chart parameter. More on this later, but here we can see that filled colors are added below the chart's line.

Simple bar charts

Bar charts are typically used like line charts, but they fill the full area of the chart. They also help show values to categories of information. Let's build a simple bar chart, copy the following code into a new file called bar_chart.py, and run the script:

```
# -*- coding: utf-8 -*-
import pygal

#create a new bar chart.
bar = pygal.Bar()
bar.title = 'Searches for term: sleep'
bar.x_labels = map(str, range(2011, 2015))
bar.add('Searches', [81, 88, 88, 100])
bar.render_to_file('bar_chart.svg')
```

Go to your project directory and open bar_chart.svg in your browser. Note that the code hasn't changed much beyond the data provided and the type of chart defined (in this case, it is pygal.Bar()). The following screenshot shows the results of our script:

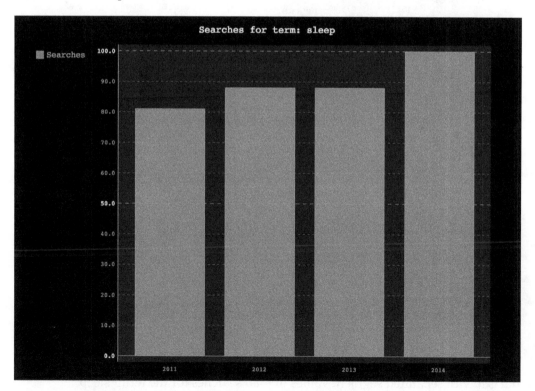

Stacked bar charts

Just like the line chart, stacked bar charts overlay different bars one over the other by data order. Let's copy the following code example and run this script:

```
# -*- coding: utf-8 -*-
import pygal

#Create a new stacked bar chart.
bar = pygal.StackedBar()
bar.title = 'Searches for term: sleep'
bar.x_labels = map(str, range(2011, 2015))
bar.add('Men', [81, 88, 88, 100])
bar.add('Women', [78, 84, 69, 92])
bar.render_to_file('bar_chart.svg')
```

The following screenshot shows the results of our script:

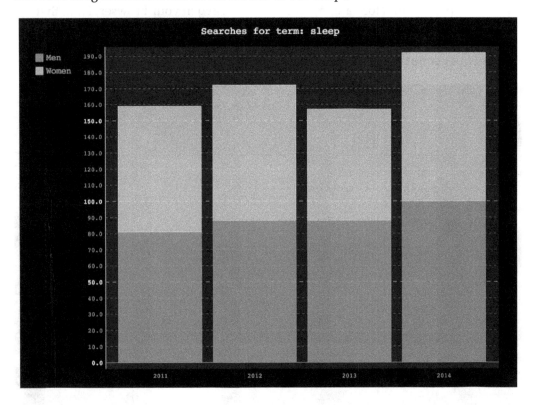

Since this is a stacked value, we have two sets of data; in this case, men and women searches. The preceding screenshot is the finished chart that shows the combined dataset with separated segment values of total searches for the term "sleep".

Horizontal bar charts

For the last bar chart type offered by pygal, we will use a horizontal chart and reuse our data from the simple bar chart. Horizontal bar charts are designed more to show data at one point in time. For this, we will remove our x_labels property since we only want a single month displayed, hence removing the years. Now, copy the following code and run the script:

```
# -*- coding: utf-8 -*-
import pygal

#create a new bar chart.
bar = pygal.HorizontalBar()
bar.title = 'Searches for term: sleep in April'
bar.add('Searches', [81, 88, 88, 100])
bar.render_to_file('bar_chart.svg')
```

Open the bar_chart.svg file; the result is shown in the following screenshot:

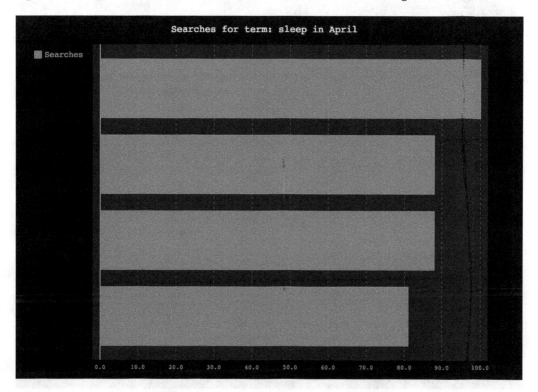

XY charts

XY charts are typically used in scientific data to show multiple values at various points. They can display negative values as well. They also overlay multiple sets of values for easy readability. Let's build a simple XY chart with two points. Copy the following code into your Python file and run the application, and save your SVG file output as xy_chart.svg:

```
# -*- coding: utf-8 -*-
import pygal

xy_chart = pygal.XY()
xy_chart.add('Value 1', [(-50, -30), (100, 45)])

xy_chart.render_to_file("xy_chart.svg")
```

Open the xy_chart.svg file; the result is shown in the following screenshot:

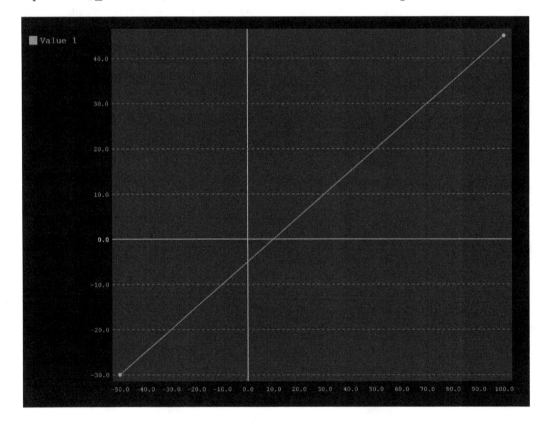

Note how `pygal` highlights the 0 lines on both the x and y coordinates; again, this is free styling provided by the `pygal` library to indicate negative values. Also, take note of the `add()` function, of how each value is noted as an (x, y) coordinate, grouped together in an array. Let's build another chart, this time with two plots; in this case, we build with `Value 1` and `Value 2`. Copy the following code and run it:

```
# -*- coding: utf-8 -*-
import pygal

xy_chart = pygal.XY()
xy_chart.add('Value 1',  [(-50, -30), (100, 45)])
xy_chart.add('Value 2',  [(-2, -14), (370, 444)])
xy_chart.render_to_file("xy_chart.svg")
```

Open the `xy_chart.svg` file; note that two line plots are present, as shown in the following screenshot:

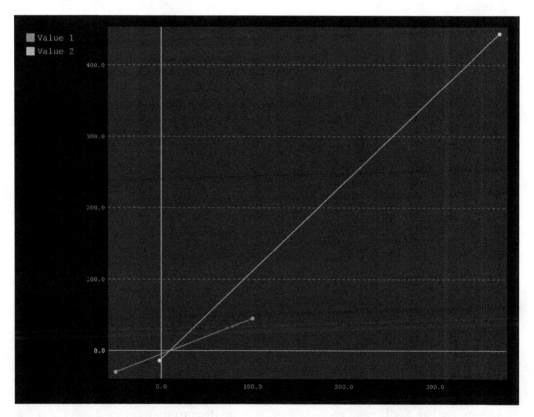

We will now see how to make a basic line plot in an XY chart, but what if we have multiple values on one line? Let's write one more XY chart with three values and six points per value. Let's look at the following code for this and run it:

```
# -*- coding: utf-8 -*-
import pygal

xy_chart = pygal.XY()
xy_chart.add('Value 1',  [(-50, -30), (100, 45), (120, 56), (168,
102), (211, 192), (279, 211)])
xy_chart.add('Value 2',  [(-2, -14), (370, 444), (391, 464), (399,
512), (412, 569), (789, 896)])
xy_chart.add('Value 3',  [(2, 10), (142, 164), (184, 216), (203, 243),
(208, 335), (243, 201)])
xy_chart.render_to_file("xy_chart.svg")
```

When it is finished, open the `xy_chart.svg` file; it should look like what is shown in the following screenshot:

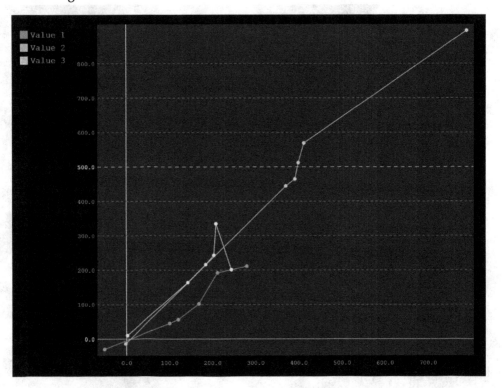

Note how we can easily read each dataset. We can discern that `Value 2` has the most values that are on the higher side, and also that `Value 3` reached a higher point than `Value 1` but dropped down quickly, which makes XY charts great for scientific data. Now, let's take a look at a variation of XY charts called scatter plots.

Scatter plots

Scatter plots work the same as XY charts, but they do not have lines that link together. In the `pygal` library, there is no "scatterplot" function to use this time. Instead, we simply reuse the XY chart function and set a parameter; in this case, `stroke` is equal to `False` (the default for `stroke` is `True`). Let's reuse our XY code from the last chart, add the `stroke` parameter, and take a look:

```
# -*- coding: utf-8 -*-
import pygal

xy_chart = pygal.XY(stroke=False)
xy_chart.add('Value 1',  [(-50, -30), (100, 45), (120, 56), (168,
102), (211, 192), (279, 211)])
xy_chart.add('Value 2',  [(-2, -14), (370, 444), (391, 464), (399,
512), (412, 569), (789, 896)])
xy_chart.add('Value 3',  [(2, 10), (142, 164), (184, 216), (203, 243),
(208, 335), (243, 201)])
xy_chart.render_to_file("xy_chart.svg")
```

Open the `xy_chart.svg` file; it should look like what's shown in the following screenshot:

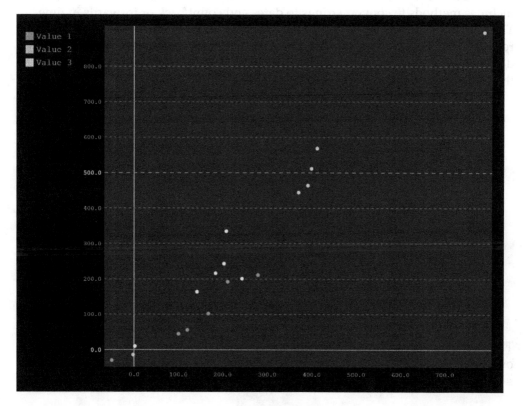

Note how this chart can be a bit easier to read with many more data points. Usually, a good rule of thumb to use XY charts versus scatter plots is if you have more than 10 points per dataset or more than 6 datasets to display. Before we wrap up this chapter, let's take a look at one more variation of the XY chart library in the `pygal` library: **DateY**.

DateY charts

DateY charts work the same as any XY chart, with one exception. Each data point is associated with a date, not a string type in Python with a date but a physical datetime object in our Python code. Each X label will be associated with a `date` object in our Python code, and Y will either be an integer or a float supplied by us.

Unlike our scatter plots, DateY does include its own function with its own rules to be followed. Let's build a very simple DateY chart to see what we are dealing with. Firstly, before running the following code, take a look at the `datetime` library, specifically `datetime` and `timedelta`.

The `datetime` library is a built-in library for Python and is pretty straightforward. It allows dates to be saved to code from the local machine's internal clock and includes methods to convert strings to dates and count back or forwards in time. The `timedelta` function belongs to the `datetime` library. What `timedelta()` represents is the duration, and the difference between two dates or times, with date-based parameters. Let's build a quick script called `timedelta.py` and copy the following code to view the result:

```
# -*- coding: utf-8 -*-
import datetime

from time import sleep
start = datetime.datetime.now()
sleep(5) #delay the python script for 5 seconds.
stop = datetime.datetime.now()

elapsed = stop - start
if elapsed > datetime.timedelta(minutes=4):
    print "Slept for greater than 4 minutes"

if elapsed > datetime.timedelta(seconds=4):
    print "Slept for greater than 4 seconds"
```

The output is shown in the following screenshot. Note that we passed 4 seconds in our script using the `sleep()` function to set a delay of 5 seconds before setting the `stop` variable's date.

The `time.sleep()` function is a common Python function and is great for process-intensive code that can't be multithreaded, such as copying or deleting files on a hard drive or setting a delay for a network activity using Python.

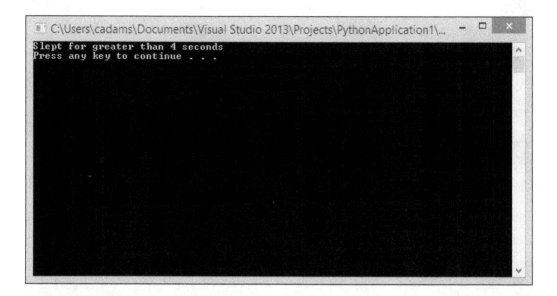

Next, let's write our DateY chart. For this chart, we will timestamp an array of dates with values; in this case, passengers arriving from St. Louis at a given time. Let's write the following code and save the output as `datey_chart.svg`:

```
# -*- coding: utf-8 -*-
import pygal
from datetime import datetime, timedelta

Date_Y = pygal.DateY()
Date_Y.title = "Flights and amount of passengers arriving from St.
Louis."
Date_Y.add("Arrival", [
    (datetime(2014, 1, 5), 42),
    (datetime(2014, 1, 14), 123),
    (datetime(2014, 2, 2), 97),
    (datetime(2014, 3, 22), 164)
])
Date_Y.render_to_file('datey_chart.svg')
```

Now, let's take a look at the following chart. We can see that a full date time is associated with each data point as well as our chart value, in this case, passengers. We can also see a range of time on the *x* axis labels. However, there is an issue with this. Take a look at the following chart and look at the labels on the x-axis:

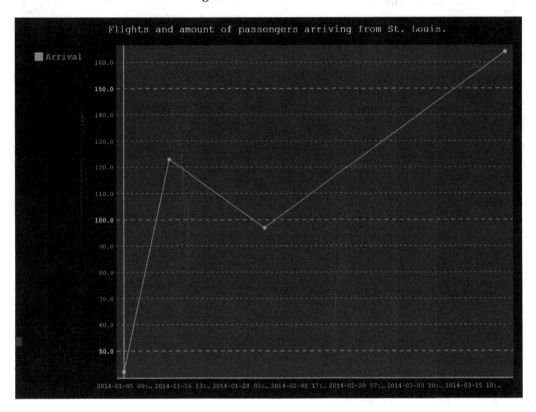

Note how the labels bunch up and crop off if they don't fit. This is not a worry for us as the DateY chart has an optional parameter to help render these labels. We can rotate them along the *x* axis using the parameter shown in the following code:

```
# -*- coding: utf-8 -*-
import pygal
from datetime import datetime, timedelta

Date_Y = pygal.DateY(x_label_rotation=25)
Date_Y.title = "Flights and amount of passengers arriving from St.
Louis."
Date_Y.add("Arrival", [
    (datetime(2014, 1, 5), 42),
```

```
        (datetime(2014, 1, 14), 123),
        (datetime(2014, 2, 2), 97),
        (datetime(2014, 3, 22), 164)
    ])
Date_Y.render_to_file('datey_chart.svg')
```

Now, let's re-render our chart as shown in the following screenshot. We can see that the labels are formatted in a way that helps with readability:

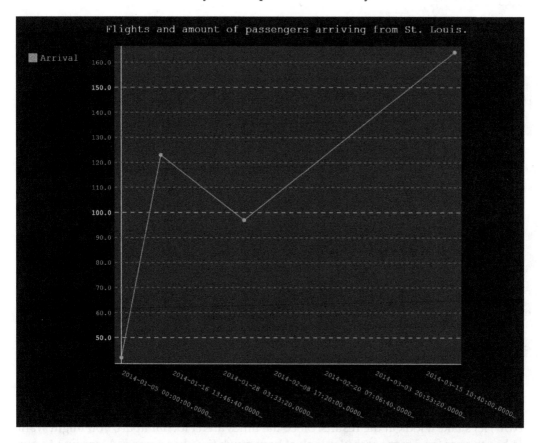

Let's add one more chart before we finish this chapter. Here, we're going to capture two points in time called by our code, one will be delayed with a sleep delay just like our `timedelta` example; we're going to have two flights come in at two separate points in time.

Here, we will set a delay between two arrivals and set the time for each data point. We will use `time.sleep()` to delay the script. Run the following script. Keep in mind that since the chart has a delay in its code, the SVG file will need 277 seconds to process:

```
# -*- coding: utf-8 -*-
import pygal, time
from datetime import datetime

#Set pre-defined arrival dates for compare.
arrival1 = datetime.now()
time.sleep(277)
arrival2 = datetime.now()

delta = arrival2 - arrival1
result = str(delta.seconds) + ' seconds'


Date_Y = pygal.DateY(x_label_rotation=25)
Date_Y.title = "Flights and amount of passengers arriving from St.
Louis."
Date_Y.add("Arrival", [
    (datetime(2014, 1, 5), 42),
    (datetime(2014, 1, 14), 123),
    (datetime(2014, 2, 2), 97),
    (datetime(2014, 3, 22), 164)
])
Date_Y.add("Arrivals today (time between flights %s)" % result, [
(arrival1, 14),
(arrival2, 47)
])

Date_Y.render_to_file('datey_chart.svg')
```

Now, let's take a look at the results. Since the times aren't too far apart, you might want to hover over for a more granular look at how much time has passed. According to our label, 277 seconds have passed:

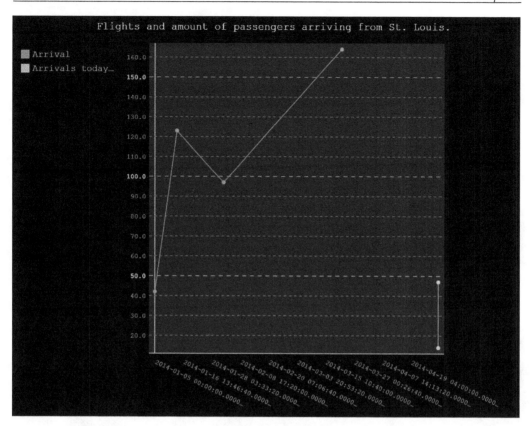

Summary

Well done! You've completed the first round of charts using the `pygal` library! We reviewed common charts, such as line and bar charts, scatter plots, and XY charts; learned about using charts with DateY, including comparisons between two `datetime` variables; and created a chart that simulated a real-world scenario.

If you struggled with this chapter, that's okay. Just begin to work through the first few charts (the line and bar charts), and create some of your own graphs with your own data until you get more confident.

In the next chapter, we will cover much more advanced chart types in the `pygal` library, including world maps, with much more complex data.

4
Advanced Charts

In this chapter, we will explore and build some more advanced SVG charts using the **pygal** charting library for Python. We will also explore the worldmap chart with pygal and explore data types that are specific to that chart.

Pie charts

Pie charts work well with displaying data of a group or the total sum of a set of data, which is broken out like a pie. Let's build a simple pie chart with some dummy data. Take a look at the following code and incorporate it into your own Python file. Note that we are saving the file output to `pie_chart.svg` this time:

```
# -*- coding: utf-8 -*-
import pygal

pie_chart = pygal.Pie()
pie_chart.title = 'Total top tablet sales in 2013 (in %)'
pie_chart.add('iPad & iPad mini', 49.7)
pie_chart.add('Surface Pro 2', 36.3)
pie_chart.add('Surface 2', 24.5)
pie_chart.add('Nexus 7', 17.5)

pie_chart.render_to_file('pie_chart.svg')
```

The following screenshot shows you the results of our script:

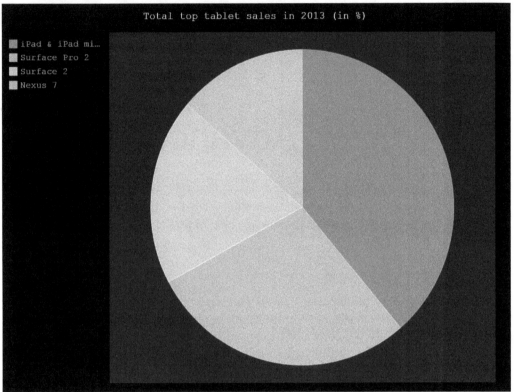

As we can see in the preceding chart, each `add()` function to the pie chart adds a different device as a slice to the pie chart. The `pie` function also includes our standard legend based on the string given in our first parameter.

Stacked pie charts

Stacked pie charts work just as they sound; they stack values in each slice of the pie chart, giving you a more in-depth look at data. As stacked charts can include multiple values that aren't a part of the pie as a whole, we will build this chart without checking for errors. Let's build our chart with the following code sample; notice that we are still using the `Pie()` function, which is similar to our scatter plot and XY charts from the previous chapter. One limitation is that stacked pie charts in pygal only accept one other value on top of the main value. We can also use single values as shown on the Nexus 7 dataset. This is shown in the following code:

```
# -*- coding: utf-8 -*-
import pygal
```

```
pie_chart = pygal.Pie()
pie_chart.title = 'Total top tablet sales in 2013 (in %)'
pie_chart.add('iPad & iPad mini', [19.7, 21.3])
pie_chart.add('Surface 2 (& Pro 2)', [24.5, 36.3])
pie_chart.add('Nexus 7', 17.5)

pie_chart.render_to_file('pie_chart.svg')
```

Open the pie_chart.svg file and the result will be as shown in the following screenshot:

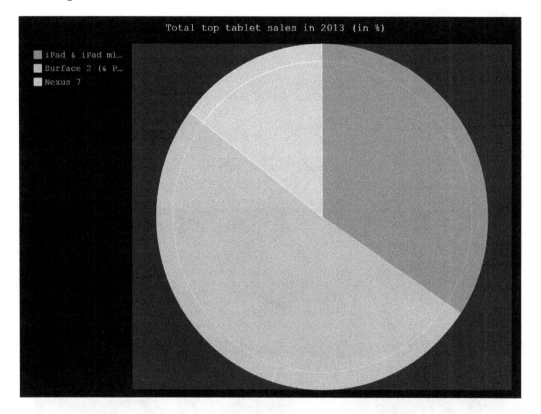

In the preceding example, we can see the sublayer slices within each pie slice. Taking a look at our code sample, notice that the extra slice comes from the Python list array inside our second parameter for each add() function that we add to our chart object.

Radar charts

Radar charts are great at displaying multiple variables for one data object. Radar charts typically look like what you would expect to see on a radar at an airport, showing you a map area with a zero point in the middle. A common place you can find radar charts in is the application performance. They have also been used in sports charts, displaying a player's or team's strengths and weaknesses. For this chart, we will build a budget estimate and the actual budget spend for a single project combined in one chart:

```
# -*- coding: utf-8 -*-
import pygal

radar_chart = pygal.Radar()
radar_chart.title = 'Product Budget Figures'
radar_chart.x_labels = ['Sales', 'Marketing', 'Development', 'Customer
support', 'Information Technology', 'Administration']
radar_chart.add('Estimate', [40, 20, 100, 20, 30, 20, 10])
radar_chart.add('Actual Spending', [70, 50, 40, 10, 17, 8, 10])
radar_chart.render_to_file('radar_chart.svg')
```

Open the radar_chart.svg file, and the result will be as shown in the following screenshot:

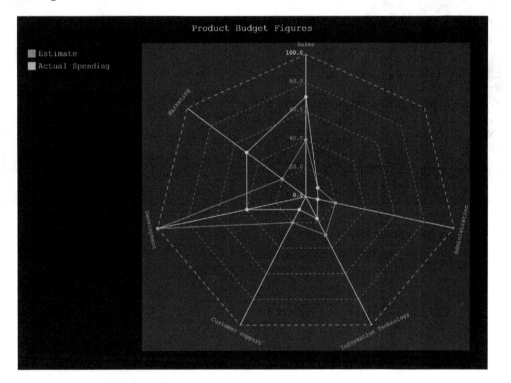

Take note of the x_labels shown in the previous code. In this case, we have Sales, Marketing, Development, Customer support, Information Technology, and Administration as one array item.

The order of each item in the array is important, as the radar chart sets the value for each dataset in the order of the array, setting that label to each endpoint of the radar in a counter-clockwise fashion. Keep this in mind when building radar charts.

Box plots

Box plots, sometimes called box and whisker plots, are a type of graph that shows you a low, medium, and high range in a value in a bar chart-like way. Box plots typically contain a box that is defined as the high range of the data then tapers on top and bottom vertically to lines indicating medium values, and the smallest values at the lines at the end of the box plot are also called whiskers.

Box plots work well with estimated values over a given range of time or supply. They also work well to show you data distribution. Box plots also use arrays for data, like in our radar chart. Let's build a simple box plot showing the cost of whole milk during the start of 2014 using the following code. Ensure that you use box_plot.svg as the filename in your render_to_file() function, as shown in the following code:

```
# -*- coding: utf-8 -*-
import pygal

box_plot = pygal.Box()
box_plot.title = 'Cost of Whole Milk in early 2014'
box_plot.add('US Dollars', [2.08, 3.14, 3.89, 3.91, 3.94, 3.98])

box_plot.render_to_file('box_plot.svg')
```

This is a pretty simple pygal chart; let's look at our example:

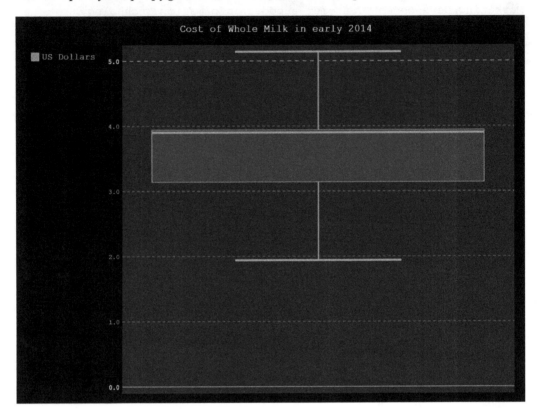

With box plots, we can add more than one box plot to the chart. Let's do that and see the results by adding another currency market. In this case, we will use Pound sterling. Copy the following code, and see the results:

```
# -*- coding: utf-8 -*-
import pygal

box_plot = pygal.Box()
box_plot.title = 'Cost of Whole Milk in early 2014'
box_plot.add('US Dollars', [2.08, 3.14, 3.89, 3.91, 3.94, 3.98])
box_plot.add('Pound Sterling', [2.78, 3.84, 1.69, 4.71, 4.84, 4.92])

box_plot.render_to_file('box_plot.svg')
```

The following screenshot shows the results of our script:

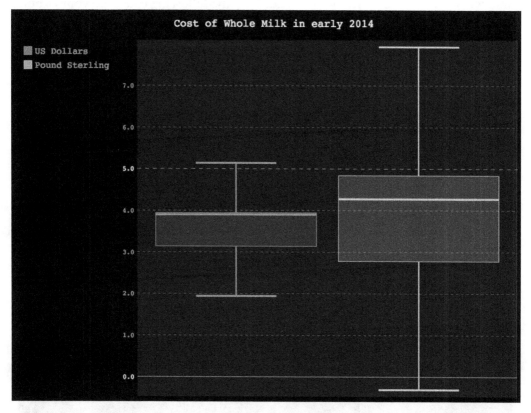

Now, with this example, we can see and compare medians of the box plots and notice, by hovering our mouse over our SVG chart, that the median for the US Dollar falls near the top of range and has remained constant, while the Pound's median is set in the middle-to-high range of the box plot, thereby showing some variation.

Dot charts

Dot charts (also known as dot plots) are similar to old computer punch cards. They are a very simple form of conveying datasets and can be an alternative to pie or bar charts. In pygal, the `dot_chart` class allows each dot to be resized based on the given value, with no extra code from the programmer. This keeps the data simple but allows the data to still be interesting to a consumer of the chart data. Commonly, you can find dot charts in datasets, also used in bar charts and allows for even easier reading of small sets of data. Some voter registration and/or statistics will use dot charts and punch in a result to a line on a card or a piece of paper.

Let's build a simple dot chart. We will reuse the datasets from our box plot charts. First, we will use the US currency dataset. Copy the following code into your editor of choice, and ensure that you save your file as dot_chart.svg:

```
# -*- coding: utf-8 -*-
import pygal

dot_chart = pygal.Dot()
dot_chart.title = 'Cost of Whole Milk in early 2014'
dot_chart.add('US Dollars', [2.08, 3.14, 3.89, 3.91, 3.94, 3.98])

dot_chart.render_to_file('dot_chart.svg')
```

 Dot charts work well with only small amounts of data with no more than 30 values per dataset. If you're considering a dataset that is bigger than 20-25, consider a bar, line, or pie chart.

Open the dot_chart.svg file, and the result will be as shown in the following screenshot:

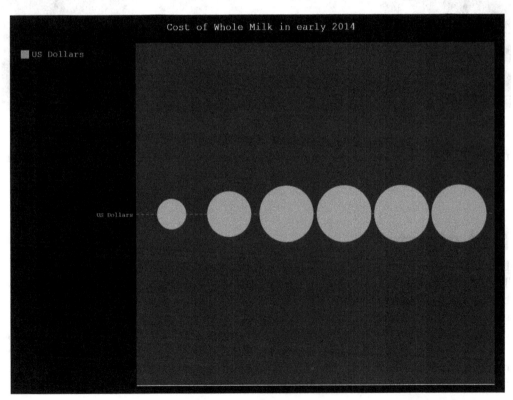

Looking at the preceding chart, you can see that the bigger the value, the bigger the dot. Traditional dot charts don't resize the dots, usually; they are kept a consistent size.

Let's add our Pound Sterling dataset from our box chart example and update the variable. We will also add the months in order to better clarify our chart using the x_labels property, and we will also add in a rotation to our *x* axis. This will add a slight rotation to our labels that will appear to overlap each other with multiple datasets. Copy the following code:

```
# -*- coding: utf-8 -*-
import pygal

dot_chart = pygal.Dot(x_label_rotation=45)
dot_chart.title = 'Cost of Whole Milk in early 2014'
dot_chart.x_labels = ['Jan', 'Feb', 'Mar', 'April', 'May', 'June']
dot_chart.add('US Dollars', [2.08, 3.14, 3.89, 3.91, 3.94, 3.98])
dot_chart.add('Pound Sterling', [2.78, 3.84, 1.69, 4.71, 4.84, 4.92])

dot_chart.render_to_file('dot_chart.svg')
```

Open the dot_chart.svg file and the result will be as shown in the following screenshot:

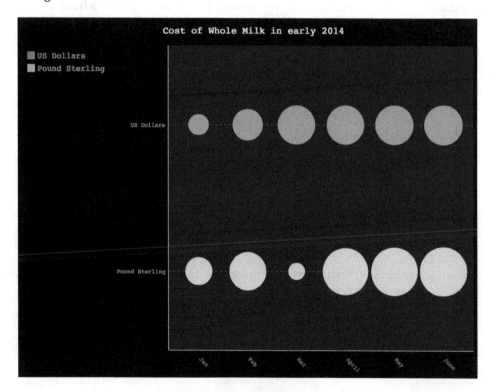

Here, with the x axis labels, we now have a better understanding of data across datasets. This looks pretty good, and with the resizing dots, we can see general values for each month.

 Dot charts are easy to build with a library, but building them from scratch from libraries is not. The issue is to create a properly sized dot, as each data value requires a great deal of mathematical knowledge. Be forewarned of this if you attempt to build or restyle a library with dot charts.

Funnel charts

Funnel charts (also known as funnel plots) are a type of graph that highlight certain shared properties of some stages in the data in which datasets come from multiple data sources, but seem to overlap each other across one central point. Typically, these charts are intended to show you a commonality around a group of datasets.

One advantage of funnel charts in pygal is that they work well, displaying data with large value sets, for instance, aeronautics and rocket science, being able to test and read data of airspeed, pounds of fuel used for thrust, and so on. Let's take a look at an example with a chart like those mentioned previously; here, we have a code sample that shows us the amount of thrust used by a space shuttle over the time of takeoff. Copy the following code, and let's run this code sample in our editor of choice. Again, ensure that you save this in a separate chart name, this time, `funnel_chart.svg`. We will also add an `x_label_rotation` property to the chart in order to help show our datasets:

```
# -*- coding: utf-8 -*-
import pygal

funnel_chart = pygal.Funnel(x_label_rotation=40)
funnel_chart.title = 'Amount of thrust used in a space shuttle at
takeoff (in lbs)'
funnel_chart.x_labels = ['Pre-takeoff', '5 min', ' 10 min', '15 min',
'20 min']
funnel_chart.add('Main Engine', [7000000, 6115200, 5009600, 4347400,
2341211])
funnel_chart.add('Engine #1', [1285000, 1072000, 89000, 51600, 12960])
funnel_chart.add('Engine #3 & #4 (mid-size)', [99000, 61600, 21960,
17856, 11235])

funnel_chart.render_to_file('funnel_chart.svg')
```

Open the `funnel_chart.svg` file, and the result will be as shown in the following screenshot:

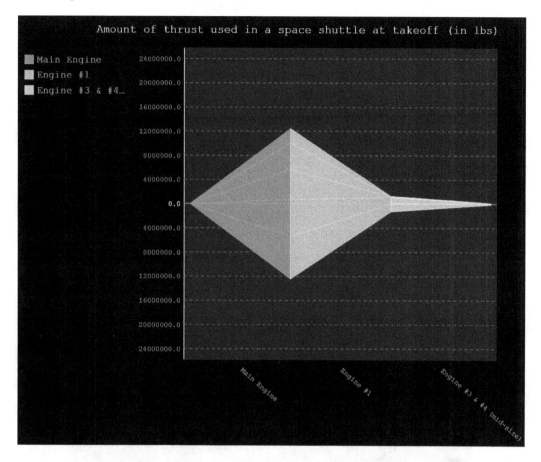

Take a look at our chart. On the *x* axis, where `Main Engine` ends and `Engine #1` takes over, we can see a tapered amount of thrust as we reach different stages from launch. Then, we see the `Main Engine` separation, and then we see the burning `Engine #1`, followed by `Engine #3 & #4`, after `Engine #1` is disengaged. This, of course, shows us space shuttle points at the time of launch and the initial thrust output when heading to space.

Gauge charts

Gauge charts display data in a graph style that is similar to speedometers in automobiles. They also work well with multiple datasets but not one with a single dataset. In the following code, we have an example of a gauge chart, which is a very simple pygal chart. This time, we will use some new data; in this case, we will use a dataset that represents the space shuttle speed from the time of launch to 20 minutes.

Let's look at our sample code and our chart in the following code snippet. Copy the code into your editor of choice, and ensure that you save the file to `gauge_chart.svg`:

```
# -*- coding: utf-8 -*-
import pygal

gauge_chart = pygal.Gauge()
gauge_chart.title = 'Speed of space shuttle during takeoff'
gauge_chart.x_labels = ['Pre-takeoff', '5 min', ' 10 min', '15 min',
'20 min']
gauge_chart.add('Pre-takeoff', 0)
gauge_chart.add('5 min', 96)
gauge_chart.add('10 min', 167)
gauge_chart.add('15 min', 249)
gauge_chart.add('20 min', 339)

gauge_chart.render_to_file('gauge_chart.svg')
```

Open the `gauge_chart.svg` file, and the result will be as shown in the following screenshot:

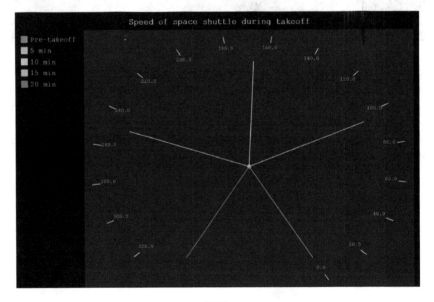

Looking at `gauge_chart.svg` in our browser, we can see a simple gauge chart. However, notice that the speed values are floats. If we are working with complex floats with multiple decimal points, we can simplify this chart and trim those floats off using `human_readable=True` in our `Gauge()` function, as shown in the following code:

```
# -*- coding: utf-8 -*-
import pygal

gauge_chart = pygal.Gauge(human_readable=True)
gauge_chart.title = 'Speed of space shuttle during takeoff'
gauge_chart.x_labels = ['Pre-takeoff', '5 min', ' 10 min', '15 min',
'20 min']
gauge_chart.add('Pre-takeoff', 0)
gauge_chart.add('5 min', 96)
gauge_chart.add('10 min', 167)
gauge_chart.add('15 min', 249)
gauge_chart.add('20 min', 339)

gauge_chart.render_to_file('gauge_chart.svg')
```

Now, let's update our chart and look at the results.

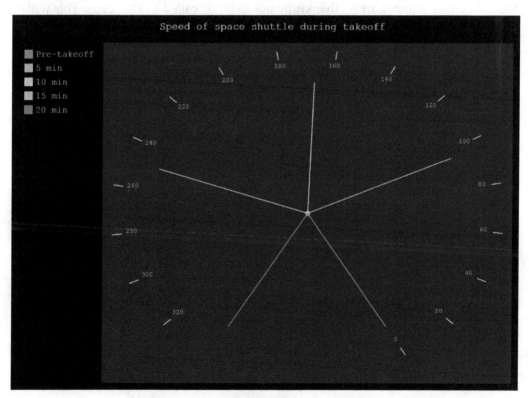

This looks good; using `human_readable=True` will help trim long values in our charts and help prevent overlapping. Notice the values in the preceding screenshot; any decimal values are now trimmed for our chart's labels.

 A neat user-interface feature of gauge charts is that if you hover over one of the values of a gauge label in a SVG-compatible browser, a dashed line will appear, indicating closeness to your dataset value.

Pyramid charts

Typically, pyramid charts are used to display large amounts of data with high data values, such as population data, voter turnout, election results, and so on.

Let's try to build a chart; now, this pygal chart will look a little different. Pyramid charts look best with lots of data, and in this case, I've typed out a bunch of data you can use to practice with. For this chart, I'm going to create an array inside of another array, with each set of parenthesis as a subarray. This will be called `miles_traveled`.

Next, I'll create another array, thankfully not as large, called `craft_type`. This will keep an array of strings that represent types of space craft, which is equal to our amount of subarrays, in this case, `Apollo Rockets`, `Russian rockets`, `US Space Shuttles`, and `Satellites`. We will also use a built-in Python function called `zip()` inside a `for` loop to iterate through our `miles_traveled`. The `zip()` function allows us to return a list of tuples or a small array of only two values:

```
# -*- coding: utf-8 -*-
import pygal


#Array of miles each with a subarray of miles traveled.
miles_traveled = [(364383, 359443, 360172, 345780, 333968, 326914,
323053, 312576, 302015, 301277, 309874, 318295, 323396, 332736,
330759, 335267, 345096, 352685, 368067, 381521, 380145, 378724,
388045, 382303, 373469, 365184, 342869, 316928, 285137, 273553,
250861, 221358, 195884, 179321, 171010, 162594, 152221, 148843,
143013, 135887, 125824, 121493, 115913, 113738, 105612, 99596, 91609,
83917, 75688, 69538, 62999, 58864, 54593, 48818, 44739, 41096, 39169,
36321, 34284, 32330, 31437, 30661, 31332, 30334, 23600, 21999, 20187,
19075, 16574, 15091, 14977, 14171, 13687, 13155, 12558, 11600, 10827,
10436, 9851, 9794, 8787, 7993, 6901, 6422, 5506, 4839, 4144, 3433,
2936, 2615),
    (349909, 340550, 342668, 346788, 319010, 312898, 308153, 296752,
289639, 290466, 296190, 303451, 309786, 317436, 315487, 316696,
325772, 331694, 345815, 354696, 354899, 351727, 354579, 341702,
```

```
336421, 321116, 292261, 261874, 242407, 229488, 208939, 184147,
162662, 147361, 140424, 134336, 126929, 125404, 122764, 116004,
105590, 100813, 95021, 90950, 85036, 79391, 72952, 66022, 59126,
52716, 46582, 42772, 38509, 34048, 30887, 28053, 26152, 23931, 22039,
20677, 19869, 19026, 18757, 18308, 14458, 13685, 12942, 12323, 11033,
10183, 10628, 10803, 10655, 10482, 10202, 10166, 9939, 10138, 10007,
10174, 9997, 9465, 9028, 8806, 8450, 7941, 7253, 6698, 6267, 5773),
    (0, 0, 0, 0, 0, 0, 0, 0, 0, 0, 0, 0, 0, 0, 0, 0, 26, 81, 312,
1319, 2987, 5816, 10053, 16045, 24240, 35066, 47828, 62384, 78916,
97822, 112799, 124414, 130658, 140789, 153951, 168560, 179996, 194471,
212006, 225209, 228886, 239690, 245974, 253459, 255455, 260715,
259980, 256481, 252222, 249467, 240268, 238465, 238167, 231361,
223832, 220459, 222512, 220099, 219301, 221322, 229783, 239336,
258360, 271151, 218063, 213461, 207617, 196227, 174615, 160855,
165410, 163070, 157379, 149698, 140570, 131785, 119936, 113751,
106989, 99294, 89097, 78413, 68174, 60592, 52189, 43375, 35469, 29648,
24678, 20365),
    (0, 0, 0, 0, 0, 0, 0, 0, 0, 0, 0, 0, 0, 0, 0, 0, 72, 344, 1478,
3901, 7878, 12899, 19948, 29108, 42475, 58287, 74163, 90724, 108375,
125886, 141559, 148061, 152871, 159725, 171298, 183536, 196136,
210831, 228757, 238731, 239616, 250036, 251759, 259593, 261832,
264864, 264702, 264070, 258117, 253678, 245440, 241342, 239843,
232493, 226118, 221644, 223440, 219833, 219659, 221271, 227123,
232865, 250646, 261796, 210136, 201824, 193109, 181831, 159280,
145235, 145929, 140266, 133082, 124350, 114441, 104655, 93223, 85899,
78800, 72081, 62645, 53214, 44086, 38481, 32219, 26867, 21443, 16899,
13680, 11508),
    (0, 0, 0, 0, 0, 0, 0, 0, 0, 0, 0, 0, 0, 0, 0, 0, 6, 7, 11, 13, 31,
34, 38, 35, 45, 299, 295, 218, 247, 252, 254, 222, 307, 316, 385, 416,
463, 557, 670, 830, 889, 1025, 1149, 1356, 1488, 1835, 1929, 2130,
2362, 2494, 2884, 3160, 3487, 3916, 4196, 4619, 5032, 5709, 6347,
7288, 8139, 9344, 11002, 12809, 11504, 11918, 12927, 13642, 13298,
14015, 15751, 17445, 18591, 19682, 20969, 21629, 22549, 23619, 25288,
26293, 27038, 27039, 27070, 27750, 27244, 25905, 24357, 22561, 21794,
20595),
    (0, 0, 0, 0, 0, 0, 0, 0, 0, 0, 0, 0, 0, 0, 0, 0, 7, 9, 9, 10, 20,
34, 49, 84, 97, 368, 401, 414, 557, 654, 631, 689, 698, 858, 1031,
1120, 1263, 1614, 1882, 2137, 2516, 2923, 3132, 3741, 4259, 4930,
5320, 5948, 6548, 7463, 8309, 9142, 10321, 11167, 12062, 13317, 15238,
16706, 18236, 20336, 23407, 27024, 32502, 37334, 34454, 38080, 41811,
44490, 45247, 46830, 53616, 58798, 63224, 66841, 71086, 73654, 77334,
82062, 87314, 92207, 94603, 94113, 92753, 93174, 91812, 87757, 84255,
79723, 77536, 74173)]

#Array of miles each with a sub array of miles traveled.
craft_type = ['Apollo Rockets', 'Russian Rockets', 'US Space
Shuttles', 'Satellites']

pyramid_chart = pygal.Pyramid()
```

```
pyramid_chart.title = 'Miles traveled of earth spacecraft'

#loop thru miles_traveled for each sub-array and add them to a craft_
type as a data set.
for type, miles in zip(craft_type, miles_traveled):
    pyramid_chart.add(type, miles)

pyramid_chart.render_to_file('pyramid_chart.svg')
```

Now, let's look at our new pyramid chart in the next screenshot. We can see quite a bit of data. Each horizontal line shows you the number of miles traveled per mission, and as more of the launch time progresses, we can see the miles taper off for some of the earlier forms of space travel with satellites and shuttles using more miles.

Open the `pyramid_chart.svg` file, and the result will be as shown in the following screenshot:

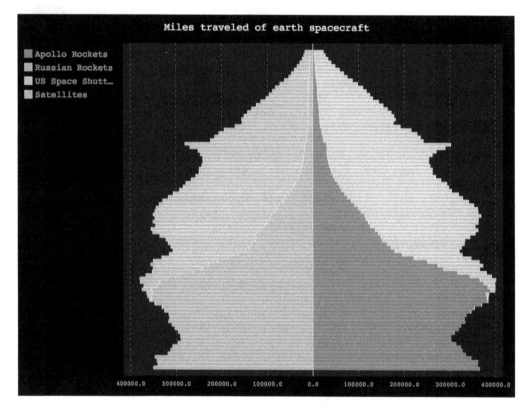

Worldmap charts

I don't think the worldmap charts need much introduction. It's a worldmap that is separated into countries, which outputs to an SVG file. The worldmap chart is a fantastic feature of the `pygal` library and is partially why I like this Python charting library. This is because not many Python charting libraries have maps as a feature, let alone ones that use the SVG output, making the map charts pygal produce very portable chart files, in our modern HTML5 mobile world we live in today.

A simple worldmap is easy to build with a little bit of dummy data using the pygal library. Let's build a simple worldmap with only United States and China highlighted as an example. Copy the following code into your editor of choice, run your Python script, and let's take a look at the results. Also, ensure that you save your output SVG file as `world_map.svg`.

```
# -*- coding: utf-8 -*-
import pygal

worldmap_chart = pygal.Worldmap()
worldmap_chart.title = 'Highlighting China and the United States'
worldmap_chart.add('China', ['cn'])
worldmap_chart.add('United States', ['us'])

#Render file.
worldmap_chart.render_to_file('world_map.svg')
```

Open the `world_map.svg` file, and the result will be as shown in the following screenshot:

So, in the preceding screenshot, we have our output worldmap, and we can verify that both `China` and `United States` are highlighted. We can also see Hawaii and Alaska properly highlighted in `United States`. Let's review our code and see what's different with the worldmap in comparison with our other charts.

Take a look at our `add()` functions for our `world_map` variable, and take a look at the two parameters passed in it, as shown in the following code:

```
worldmap_chart.add('China', ['cn'])
worldmap_chart.add('United States', ['us'])
```

Notice that our `add()` function works similar to our past chart; however, this time, we are passing in a string instead of a number inside an array, in this case, a single item array with a string. This string is actually a two-letter country code, and since it's a standard country code pygal can set values to a specific country on our map.

Going back to the array in our `add()` method, what happens if we add multiple countries to an array for a single `add()` function? Let's rework our chart in order to allow multiple countries to be highlighted.

This time, we will rename `United States` and change the label to `U.S. Allies`. Let's add these allies along with our `us` country code and see what happens. Also, I'll break our array up to a new line for each country code (each country code is taken to a new line in the code bundle) so that we can easily read or if we need to update our code:

```
# -*- coding: utf-8 -*-
import pygal

worldmap_chart = pygal.Worldmap()
worldmap_chart.title = 'United States Allies and China'
worldmap_chart.add('China', ['cn'])
worldmap_chart.add('U.S. Allies', ['al',
'be','bg','ca','hr','cz','dk','ee','ff','de','hu','is','it',
'lv','lt','lu','nl','no','pl','pt','ro','si','sk','tr','us','uk'])

#Render file.
worldmap_chart.render_to_file('world_map.svg')
```

Open the `world_map.svg` file, and the result will be as shown in the following screenshot:

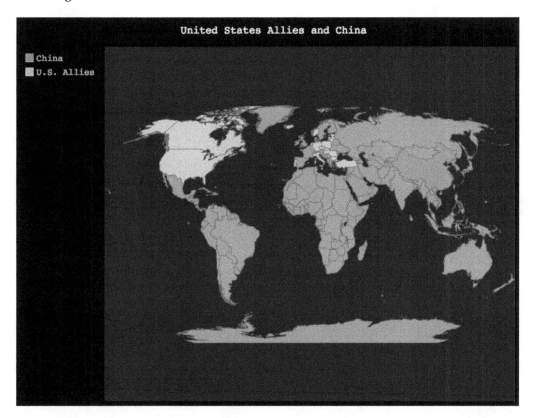

Not bad; we can easily see the chart highlighting our U.S. Allies with the same color, while China is highlighted with another color on a separate dataset.

 Worldmaps are great SVG charts. One thing to note is that worldmaps are very complex SVG images, so consider the amount of data your own charts will include, and steer clear of extremely complex datasets. Some mobile platforms that render SVGs with animations might turn out sluggish when deployed.

Summary

With that finished, this chapter comes to a close. In this chapter, we covered the remainder of the charts of the pygal library, features, and proper uses of more advanced charts and very complex datasets. At this point, consider building your own charts with your own data. Experiment and play with the results; the more you play with the library, the better your understanding of how you should structure data. In the next chapter, we will start learning about pygal themes, optional features, and customizations.

5
Tweaking pygal

In this chapter, we will cover how to apply themes and use some of the optional features used in the pygal library. We will also look at themes and styling of our charts.

Country charts

The pygal library has a chart that we didn't review in the past chapters; this is a good time to bring the topic up and discuss the chart. It's called the **country chart**. Like the worldmap chart, it shows the deeper detailed regions of a country; unfortunately, at the time of writing this book, it's limited only to the country of France, and it works pretty similar to the world map.

If you remember our introductory chapter, you might remember our discussion on Kozea, the open source community originating in France that developed the pygal library. Since they came from France, they created a map for their own country, including sectioned areas called departments and regions. France's regions are similar to states, and departments are similar to counties in a state.

Let's take a look at some sample code for this map, and we can then build on it using some extra features of pygal's frameworks. First, let's build a simple example using departments. Create a new Python file and copy the following code into your editor of choice. Notice the similarities between this and our worldmap code in *Chapter 4, Advanced Charts*. Be sure to use france_map.svg as the file output:

```
# -*- coding: utf-8 -*-
import pygal

france_chart = pygal.FrenchMap_Departments()
france_chart.title = 'Sample departments'
france_chart.add('Data-set 1', ['17'])
france_chart.add('Data-set 2', ['27'])
```

```
france_chart.add('Data-set 3', ['38'])
france_chart.add('Data-set 4', ['42'])
france_chart.add('Data-set 5', ['19'])
france_chart.render_to_file('france_map.svg')
```

Open the `france_map.svg` file, and the result will be what's shown in the following screenshot:

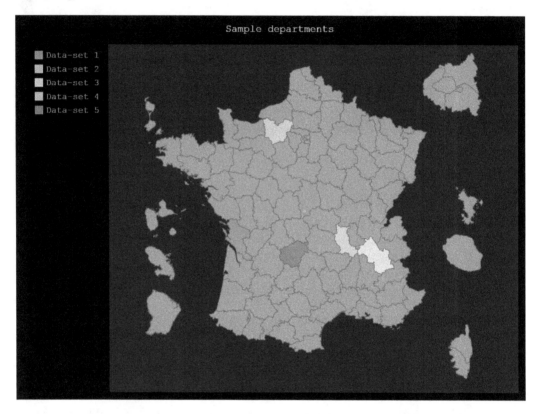

Let's take a look at our `france_chart` type. Note that we used `pygal.FrenchMap_Departments()` with our chart type suffixed with `Departments`. With this chart, there are two modes—one for departments and the other for regions. Use the following code to see how region-based charts are created. Note the suffix this time:

```
# -*- coding: utf-8 -*-
import pygal

france_chart = pygal.FrenchMap_Regions()
france_chart.title = 'Sample Regions'
france_chart.add('Centre', ['24'])
```

```
france_chart.add('Lorraine', ['41'])
france_chart.add('Picardy', ['22'])
france_chart.add('Upper Normandy', ['23'])
france_chart.add('Corsica', ['94'])
france_chart.render_to_file('france_map.svg')
```

Open the `france_map.svg` file, and the result will be what's shown in the following screenshot:

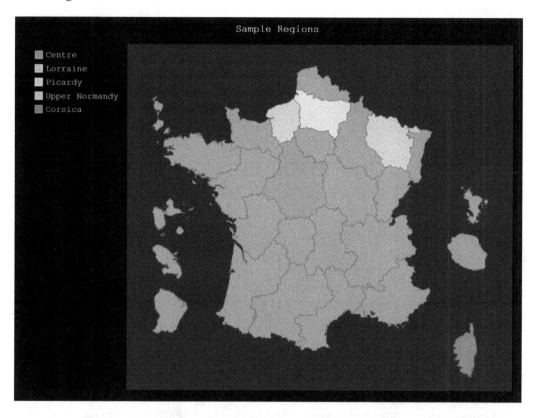

Looking closer at the code, we might wonder why we aren't using abbreviations for regions, or ask how to set our active regions or departments. The reason for the numbers is that France uses its own INSEE numbers.

Institut National de la Statistique et des Études Économiques (INSEE) is France's national institute for statistics and economics, which created the numbering system for its departments and regions. Since this is a common system to identify sections of France, the `pygal` library developers use the same numbers to assign highlights to the map chart. Now that we know how to use this chart, let's modify it this time, not with data, but with parameters, methods, and themes included in the `pygal` library.

Parameters

We have seen parameters used in our pygal-related chapters throughout the book. Here, we will start with our regions-based France chart, but first let's go ahead and fill in the rest of the regions on the chart. Copy the following code into your editor of choice and render the chart:

```
# -*- coding: utf-8 -*-
import pygal

france_chart = pygal.FrenchMap_Regions()
france_chart.title = 'Sample Regions'
france_chart.add('Alsace', ['42'])
france_chart.add('Aquitaine', ['72'])
france_chart.add('Auvergne', ['83'])
france_chart.add('Brittany', ['53'])
france_chart.add('Burgundy', ['26'])
france_chart.add('Centre', ['24'])
france_chart.add('Champagne-Ardenne', ['21'])
france_chart.add(unicode('Franche-Comté', 'utf-8'), ['43'])
france_chart.add(unicode('Île-de-France', 'utf-8'), ['11'])
france_chart.add('Languedoc-Roussillon', ['91'])
france_chart.add('Limousin', ['74'])
france_chart.add('Lorraine', ['41'])
france_chart.add('Lower Normandy', ['25'])
france_chart.add(unicode('Midi-Pyrénées', 'utf-8'), ['73'])
france_chart.add('Nord-Pas-de-Calais', ['31'])
france_chart.add('Pays de la Loire', ['52'])
france_chart.add('Picardy', ['22'])
france_chart.add('Poitou-Charentes', ['54'])
france_chart.add(unicode('Provence-Alpes-Côte d\'Azur', 'utf-8'),
['93'])
france_chart.add(unicode('Rhône-Alpes', 'utf-8'), ['83'])
france_chart.add('Upper Normandy', ['23'])
france_chart.add('Corsica', ['94'])
france_chart.add('French Guiana', ['03'])
france_chart.add('Guadeloupe', ['01'])
france_chart.add('Mayotte', ['05'])
france_chart.add('Reunion', ['04'])
france_chart.render_to_file('france_map.svg')
```

When done, you should see what is shown in the following screenshot:

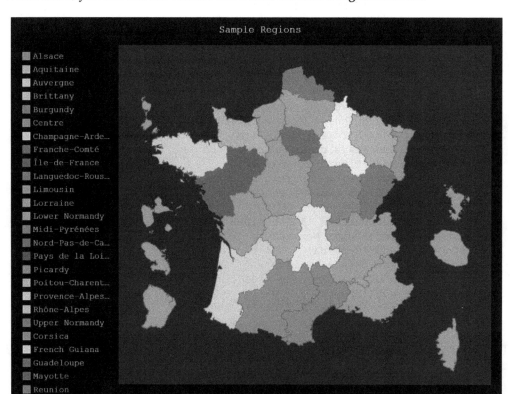

In the preceding screenshot, we can see quite a few regions in our legend. Notice how much space they take up in our chart. Let's tinker with some formatting parameters to clean this up.

Legend at the bottom

We can reposition the legend for the chart using the legend_at_bottom parameter and passing in a value either as True or False. Here's an example and the output screen. Notice the legend_at_bottom parameter in the FrenchMap_Regions() method:

```
# -*- coding: utf-8 -*-
import pygal

france_chart = pygal.FrenchMap_Regions(legend_at_bottom=True)
france_chart.title = 'Sample Regions'
france_chart.add('Alsace', ['42'])
france_chart.add('Aquitaine', ['72'])
france_chart.add('Auvergne', ['83'])
france_chart.add('Brittany', ['53'])
```

```
france_chart.add('Burgundy', ['26'])
france_chart.add('Centre', ['24'])
france_chart.add('Champagne-Ardenne', ['21'])
france_chart.add(unicode('Franche-Comté', 'utf-8'), ['43'])
france_chart.add(unicode('Île-de-France', 'utf-8'), ['11'])
france_chart.add('Languedoc-Roussillon', ['91'])
france_chart.add('Limousin', ['74'])
france_chart.add('Lorraine', ['41'])
france_chart.add('Lower Normandy', ['25'])
france_chart.add(unicode('Midi-Pyrénées', 'utf-8'), ['73'])
france_chart.add('Nord-Pas-de-Calais', ['31'])
france_chart.add('Pays de la Loire', ['52'])
france_chart.add('Picardy', ['22'])
france_chart.add('Poitou-Charentes', ['54'])
france_chart.add(unicode('Provence-Alpes-Côte d\'Azur', 'utf-8'),
['93'])
france_chart.add(unicode('Rhône-Alpes', 'utf-8'), ['83'])
france_chart.add('Upper Normandy', ['23'])
france_chart.add('Corsica', ['94'])
france_chart.add('French Guiana', ['03'])
france_chart.add('Guadeloupe', ['01'])
france_chart.add('Mayotte', ['05'])
france_chart.add('Reunion', ['04'])
france_chart.render_to_file('france_map.svg')
```

The following screenshot shows the results of our script:

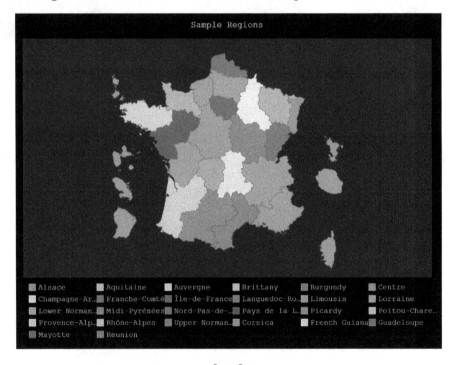

Legend settings

We can also format the legend box using the `legend_box_size` parameter which allows for an integer value; this will change the colored box sizes for each legend item. Here is an example:

```
# -*- coding: utf-8 -*-
import pygal

france_chart = pygal.FrenchMap_Regions(legend_at_bottom=True, legend_
box_size=3)
france_chart.title = 'Sample Regions'
france_chart.add('Alsace', ['42'])
france_chart.add('Aquitaine', ['72'])
france_chart.add('Auvergne', ['83'])
france_chart.add('Brittany', ['53'])
france_chart.add('Burgundy', ['26'])
france_chart.add('Centre', ['24'])
france_chart.add('Champagne-Ardenne', ['21'])
france_chart.add(unicode('Franche-Comté', 'utf-8'), ['43'])
france_chart.add(unicode('Île-de-France', 'utf-8'), ['11'])
france_chart.add('Languedoc-Roussillon', ['91'])
france_chart.add('Limousin', ['74'])
france_chart.add('Lorraine', ['41'])
france_chart.add('Lower Normandy', ['25'])
france_chart.add(unicode('Midi-Pyrénées', 'utf-8'), ['73'])
france_chart.add('Nord-Pas-de-Calais', ['31'])
france_chart.add('Pays de la Loire', ['52'])
france_chart.add('Picardy', ['22'])
france_chart.add('Poitou-Charentes', ['54'])
france_chart.add(unicode('Provence-Alpes-Côte d\'Azur', 'utf-8'),
['93'])
france_chart.add(unicode('Rhône-Alpes', 'utf-8'), ['83'])
france_chart.add('Upper Normandy', ['23'])
france_chart.add('Corsica', ['94'])
france_chart.add('French Guiana', ['03'])
france_chart.add('Guadeloupe', ['01'])
france_chart.add('Mayotte', ['05'])
france_chart.add('Reunion', ['04'])
france_chart.render_to_file('france_map.svg')
```

The following screenshot shows the results of our script:

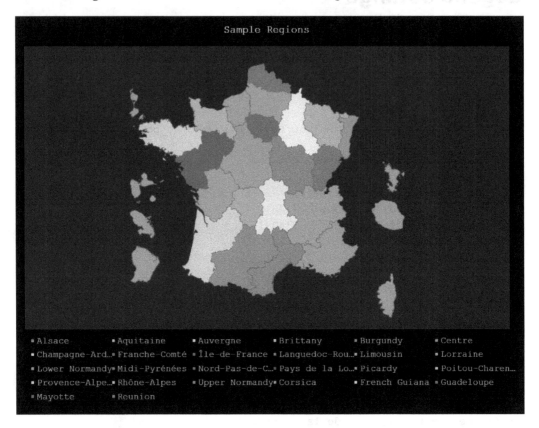

Check out how we used both the `legend_at_bottom` and `legend_box_size` parameters. We can stack them using a comma between parameters and allow many combinations. We still have an excess of labels bleeding into the next columns of the legend; let's go ahead and tweak them with these other properties.

For the next few code samples, I'll trim out the datasets so that we can focus on understanding parameters. If you need to regrab, refer to our initial chart from the *Parameters* section. Now, let's shrink down the font size of our labels and resize our boxes with the `legend_font_size` parameter:

```
# -*- coding: utf-8 -*-
import pygal

france_chart = pygal.FrenchMap_Regions(legend_at_bottom=True, legend_
box_size=8, legend_font_size=8)
# ///Data-sets (continued)
```

The following screenshot shows the results of the script:

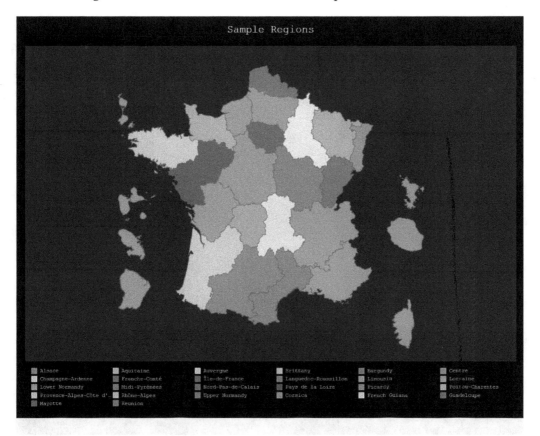

Nice! Now, one legend item is still a bit small; let's trim it along with the others for consistency, using the `truncate_legend` parameter, as shown in the following code:

```python
# -*- coding: utf-8 -*-
import pygal

france_chart = pygal.FrenchMap_Regions(legend_at_bottom=True, legend_
box_size=8, legend_font_size=8, truncate_legend=6)
```

The following screenshot shows the results of our script:

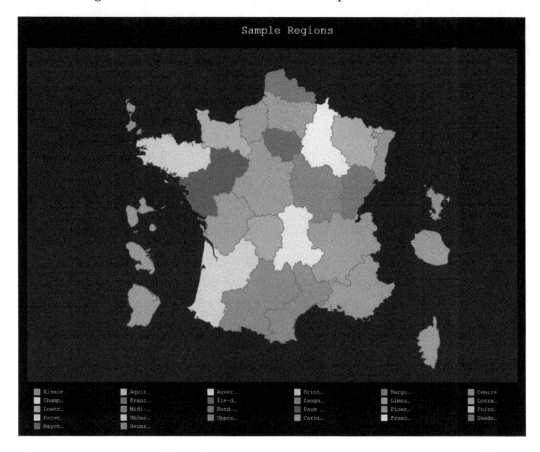

Well done! This is now looking more and more organized. We can even disable the `legend_at_bottom` parameter by either removing or setting it to `False`. It will look something like what is shown in the following screenshot:

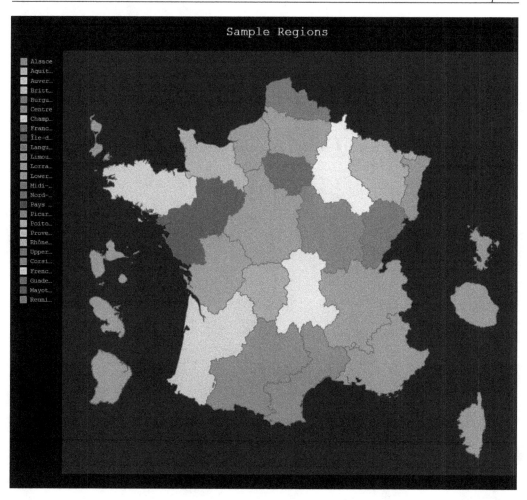

One more thing to note about legends is that you can disable them if you don't need them. Keep in mind that chart legends help users of the charts to help consume the data. Since we don't have an x and y axes labels, we should be fine to disable the legend. To do this, you just need to set the show_legend parameter to False, as shown in the following code:

```
# -*- coding: utf-8 -*-
import pygal

france_chart = pygal.FrenchMap_Regions(show_legend=False, legend_box_
size=8, legend_font_size=8, truncate_legend=6)
```

The following screenshot shows the results of our script, without a legend:

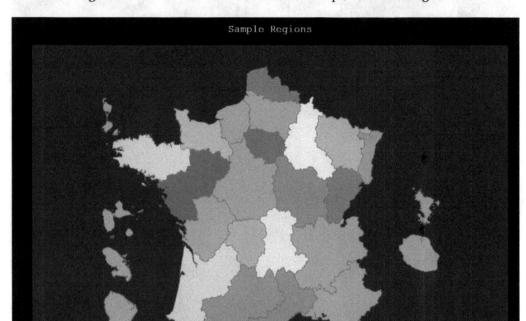

Excellent! Now, we've modified the legend to allow greater flexibility for our charts.

Label settings

Let's take a look at a traditional line chart where we can use labels. Here's a simple chart with some dummy datasets. Copy the code into your editor of choice and run the script. Your output should be what is shown in the next screenshot.

You can also set label settings using similar parameters used with our legend. Let's build a simple line chart that we can see our changes on. Add the following code to an editor of your choice and run the script. Be sure to save the output as lineparam.svg:

```
# -*- coding: utf-8 -*-
import pygal

param_line_chart = pygal.Line()
```

```
param_line_chart.title = 'Parameter Line Chart'
param_line_chart.x_labels = map(str, ["Data Object 1", "Data Object
2", "Data Object 3", "Data Object 4", "Data Object 5", "Data Object
6"])
param_line_chart.add('Data-Set 1', [8, 16, 24, 32, 48, 56])
param_line_chart.add('Data-Set 2', [2, 4, 6, 8, 10, 12])
param_line_chart.add('Data-Set 3', [1, 3, 5, 7, 9, 12])

param_line_chart.render_to_file('lineparam.svg')
```

The following screenshot shows the results of our script:

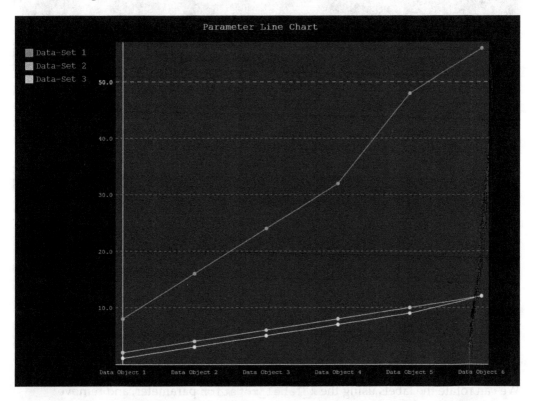

Line charts have some specific parameters, such as fill=true, as mentioned in
Chapter 3, Getting Started with pygal. You can also resize the specified labels using
the label_font_size parameter, as shown in the following code:

```
# -*- coding: utf-8 -*-
import pygal

param_line_chart = pygal.Line(fill=True, label_font_size=20)
param_line_chart.title = 'Parameter Line Chart'
```

```
param_line_chart.x_labels = map(str, ["Data Object 1", "Data Object
2", "Data Object 3", "Data Object 4", "Data Object 5", "Data Object
6"])
param_line_chart.add('Data-Set 1', [8, 16, 24, 32, 48, 56])
param_line_chart.add('Data-Set 2', [2, 4, 6, 8, 10, 12])
param_line_chart.add('Data-Set 3', [1, 3, 5, 7, 9, 12])

param_line_chart.render_to_file('lineparam.svg')
```

The following screenshot shows the results of our script:

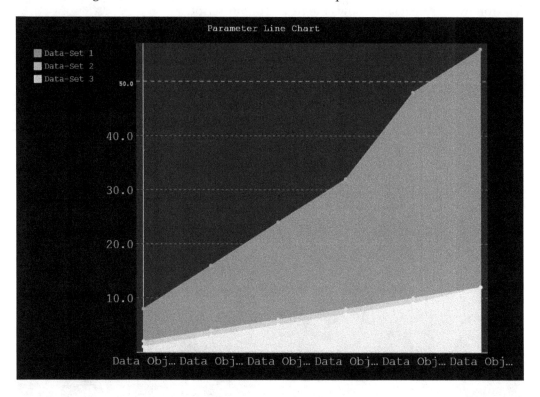

We can rotate the labels using the x_label_rotation parameter, and remove the lines all together using the stroke=false parameter, as shown in the following code:

```
# -*- coding: utf-8 -*-
import pygal

param_line_chart = pygal.Line(fill=False, stroke=False, label_font_
size=20, x_label_rotation=50)
param_line_chart.title = 'Parameter Line Chart'
```

```
param_line_chart.x_labels = map(str, ["Data Object 1", "Data Object
2", "Data Object 3", "Data Object 4", "Data Object 5", "Data Object
6"])
param_line_chart.add('Data-Set 1', [8, 16, 24, 32, 48, 56])
param_line_chart.add('Data-Set 2', [2, 4, 6, 8, 10, 12])
param_line_chart.add('Data-Set 3', [1, 3, 5, 7, 9, 12])

param_line_chart.render_to_file('lineparam.svg')
```

The following screenshot shows the results of our script:

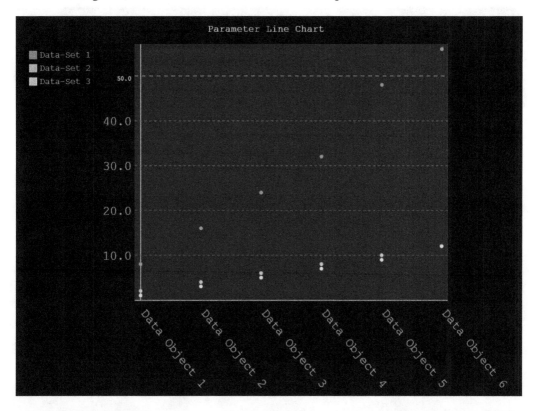

Line charts have one specific parameter, `interpolate='cubic'`, which allows the line to curve in the data. Here's an example:

```
# -*- coding: utf-8 -*-
import pygal

param_line_chart = pygal.Line(interpolate='cubic', label_font_size=20,
x_label_rotation=50)
param_line_chart.title = 'Parameter Line Chart'
```

```
param_line_chart.x_labels = map(str, ["Data Object 1", "Data Object
2", "Data Object 3", "Data Object 4", "Data Object 5", "Data Object
6"])
param_line_chart.add('Data-Set 1', [8, 16, 24, 32, 48, 56])
param_line_chart.add('Data-Set 2', [2, 4, 6, 8, 10, 12])
param_line_chart.add('Data-Set 3', [1, 3, 5, 7, 9, 12])

param_line_chart.render_to_file('lineparam.svg')
```

The following screenshot shows the results of our script:

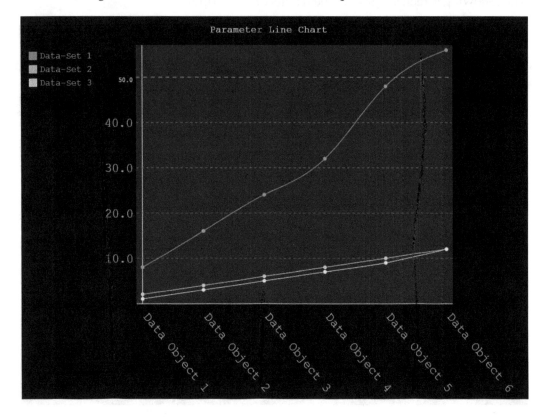

Chart title settings

We are pretty familiar with chart titles from the past two chapters, but it is good to know that we can also give titles to the *x* and *y* axes. Take a look at the following code:

```
# -*- coding: utf-8 -*-
import pygal

param_line_chart = pygal.Line(interpolate='cubic', label_font_size=20,
x_label_rotation=50)
```

```
param_line_chart.title = 'Parameter Line Chart'
param_line_chart.x_title='Data-Sets (X Axis)'
param_line_chart.y_title='Values (Y Axis)'

param_line_chart.x_labels = map(str, ["Data Object 1", "Data Object
2", "Data Object 3", "Data Object 4", "Data Object 5", "Data Object
6"])


param_line_chart.add('Data-Set 1', [8, 16, 24, 32, 48, 56])
param_line_chart.add('Data-Set 2', [2, 4, 6, 8, 10, 12])
param_line_chart.add('Data-Set 3', [1, 3, 5, 7, 9, 12])

param_line_chart.render_to_file('lineparam.svg')
```

The following screenshot shows the results of our script:

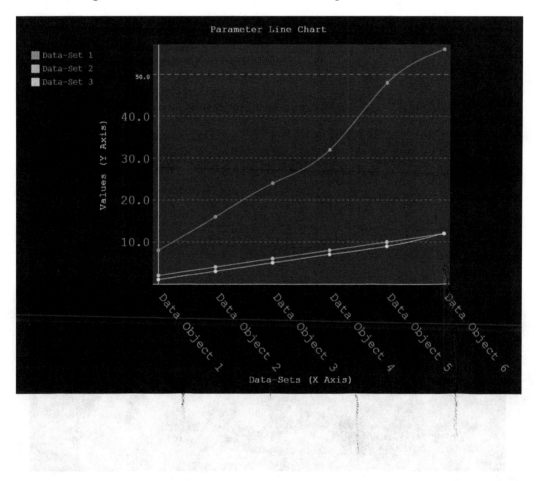

We can adjust the font sizes for the x, y, and chart titles using the `title_font_size`, `x_title_font_size`, and `y_title_font_size` parameters, as shown in the following code:

```
# -*- coding: utf-8 -*-
import pygal

param_line_chart = pygal.Line(interpolate='cubic', label_font_size=20,
x_label_rotation=50, title_font_size=24, x_title_font_size=24, y_
title_font_size=24)
param_line_chart.title = 'Parameter Line Chart'
param_line_chart.x_title='Data-Sets (X Axis)'
param_line_chart.y_title='Values (Y Axis)'

param_line_chart.x_labels = map(str, ["Data Object 1", "Data Object
2", "Data Object 3", "Data Object 4", "Data Object 5", "Data Object
6"])

param_line_chart.add('Data-Set 1', [8, 16, 24, 32, 48, 56])
param_line_chart.add('Data-Set 2', [2, 4, 6, 8, 10, 12])
param_line_chart.add('Data-Set 3', [1, 3, 5, 7, 9, 12])

param_line_chart.render_to_file('lineparam.svg')
```

The following screenshot shows the results of our script:

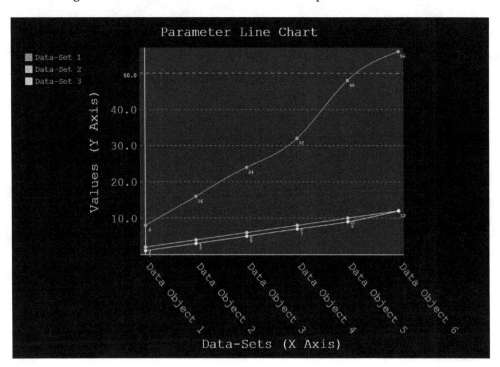

Displaying no data

One parameter worth looking at is the `no_data_text` parameter, which allows us to set a text overlay for our chart, just in case we create a chart without loading data. This is helpful if we are building a dynamic chart where we pull data from a data source, either online or locally, through a file or command-line parameters. Here's an example of the `no_data_text` parameter in action:

```
# -*- coding: utf-8 -*-
import pygal

param_line_chart = pygal.Line(no_data_text='Unable to load data')
param_line_chart.title = 'Parameter Line Chart'
param_line_chart.x_title='Data-Sets (X Axis)'
param_line_chart.y_title='Values (Y Axis)'

param_line_chart.x_labels = map(str, ["Data Object 1", "Data Object
2", "Data Object 3", "Data Object 4", "Data Object 5", "Data Object
6"])

#param_line_chart.add('Data-Set 1', [8, 16, 24, 32, 48, 56])
#param_line_chart.add('Data-Set 2', [2, 4, 6, 8, 10, 12])
#param_line_chart.add('Data-Set 3', [1, 3, 5, 7, 9, 12])

param_line_chart.render_to_file('lineparam.svg')
```

The following screenshot shows the results of our script:

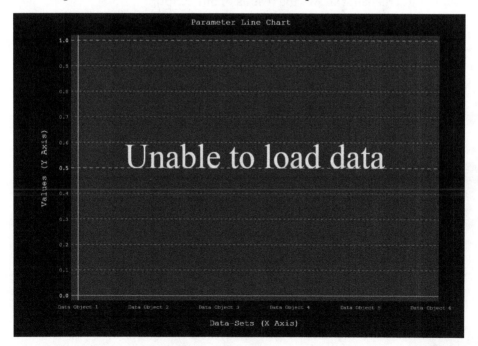

pygal themes

So far, we have used the default theme, known simply as **Default**, for pygal charts. However, pygal offers 14 prebuilt themes. Let's update our line chart code with another theme called **Neon**:

```
# -*- coding: utf-8 -*-
import pygal
from pygal.style import NeonStyle

param_line_chart = pygal.Line(interpolate='cubic', fill=True,
style=NeonStyle)
param_line_chart.title = 'Parameter Line Chart'
param_line_chart.x_title='Data-Sets (X Axis)'
param_line_chart.y_title='Values (Y Axis)'

param_line_chart.x_labels = map(str, ["Data Object 1", "Data Object
2", "Data Object 3", "Data Object 4", "Data Object 5", "Data Object
6"])

param_line_chart.add('Data-Set 1', [8, 16, 24, 32, 48, 56])
param_line_chart.add('Data-Set 2', [2, 4, 6, 8, 10, 12])
param_line_chart.add('Data-Set 3', [1, 3, 5, 7, 9, 12])

param_line_chart.render_to_file('lineparam.svg')
```

The following screenshot shows the results of our script:

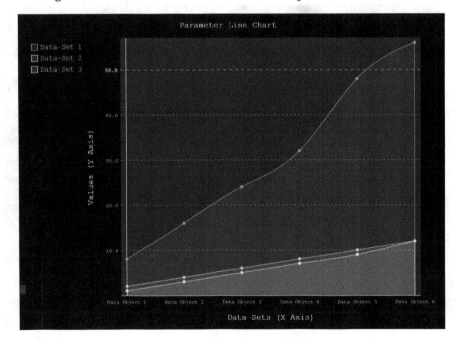

As we can see, the Neon style is similar to the Default style; however, compared to our earlier `fill` parameter using the Default style, the `fill` parameter of the Neon style has a slight transparency applied. Also, if we check our code, we will see that the style is simply a parameter applied to the chart instance with a suffix of *Style* after the name of the style selected; for the full list of themes in pygal, check out the framework documentation on themes at http://pygal.org/builtin_styles/.

Also, take a look at the line below `import pygal` in the previous code, which reads from the line `pygal.style import NeonStyle`. By default, the built-in styles are not included with our `import pygal` statement, so we need to add them, and in this case, we specify that we want to import the `NeonStyle` theme. Let's try a lighter style using the **Red Blue** theme and override our `NeonStyle`, both in our `import` and `style` parameters, as shown in the following code:

```
# -*- coding: utf-8 -*-
import pygal
from pygal.style import RedBlueStyle

param_line_chart = pygal.Line(interpolate='cubic', fill=True,
style=RedBlueStyle)
param_line_chart.title = 'Parameter Line Chart'
param_line_chart.x_title='Data-Sets (X Axis)'
param_line_chart.y_title='Values (Y Axis)'

param_line_chart.x_labels = map(str, ["Data Object 1", "Data Object
2", "Data Object 3", "Data Object 4", "Data Object 5", "Data Object
6"])

param_line_chart.add('Data-Set 1', [8, 16, 24, 32, 48, 56])
param_line_chart.add('Data-Set 2', [2, 4, 6, 8, 10, 12])
param_line_chart.add('Data-Set 3', [1, 3, 5, 7, 9, 12])

param_line_chart.render_to_file('lineparam.svg')
```

The following screenshot shows the results of our script:

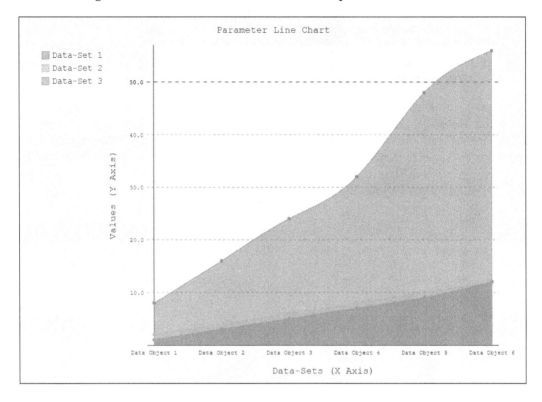

Looks good! If you're curious about finding a specific theme, refer to pygal's website for full documentation on themes at `http://pygal.org/styles/`. You can also test themes online using pygal's style tool at `http://cabaret.pygal.org/`.

Summary

In this chapter, we covered quite a bit on pygal, and we should have a pretty good handle of working with pygal building charts and modifying them to what we need. In the next chapter, we will take a break from charting and start working with the data side of building dynamic charts.

6
Importing Dynamic Data

Since we now have an understanding of how to work with the `pygal` library and building charts and graphics in general, this is the time to start looking at building an application using Python.

In this chapter, we will take a look at the fundamentals of pulling data from the Web, parsing the data, and adding it to our code base and formatting the data into a useable format, and we will look at how to carry those fundamentals over to our Python code. We will also cover parsing XML and JSON data.

Pulling data from the Web

For many non-developers, it may seem like witchcraft that developers are magically able to pull data from an online resource and integrate that with an iPhone app, or a Windows Store app, or pull data to a cloud resource that is able to generate various versions of the data upon request.

To be fair, they do have a general understanding; data is pulled from the Web and formatted to their app of choice. They just may not get the full background of how that process workflow happens. It's the same case with some developers as well—many developers mainly work on a technology that only works on a locked down environment, or generally, don't use the Internet for their applications. Again, they understand the logic behind it; somehow an RSS feed gets pulled into an application.

In many languages, the same task is done in various ways, usually depending on which language is used. Let's take a look at a few examples using Packt's own news RSS feed, using an iOS app pulling in data via Objective-C.

Now, if you're reading this and not familiar with Objective-C, that's OK, the important thing is that we have the inner XML contents of an XML file showing up in an iPhone application:

```objc
#import "ViewController.h"

@interfaceViewController ()
@property (weak, nonatomic) IBOutletUITextView *output;

@end

@implementationViewController

- (void)viewDidLoad
{
    [super viewDidLoad];
    // Do any additional setup after loading the view, typically from
a nib.

    NSURL *packtURL = [NSURLURLWithString:@"http://www.packtpub.com/
rss.xml"];
    NSURLRequest *request = [NSURLRequestrequestWithURL:packtURL];
    NSURLConnection *connection = [[NSURLConnectionalloc] initWithRequ
est:requestdelegate:selfstartImmediately:YES];

    [connection start];
}

- (void)connection:(NSURLConnection *)connection
didReceiveData:(NSData *)data {
    NSString *downloadstring = [[NSStringalloc] initWithData:dataencod
ing:NSUTF8StringEncoding];

    [self.outputsetText:downloadstring];

}


- (void)didReceiveMemoryWarning
{
    [superdidReceiveMemoryWarning];
    // Dispose of any resources that can be recreated.
}

@end
```

Here, we can see in iPhone Simulator that our XML output is pulled dynamically through HTTP from the Web to our iPhone simulator. This is what we'll want to get started with doing in Python:

```
Carrier 📶                2:36 PM                    ▬

<?xml version="1.0" encoding="utf-8" ?>
<rss version="2.0" >
 <channel>
  <title>Packt Publishing | Feed</title>
  <description>Packt Publishing special offers,
news, and contributed articles by the technical
community.</description>
  <link>http://www.packtpub.com</link>
  <item>
  <title>Master the advanced features of
CryENGINE with Packt's new book and eBook
</title>
<description></description>
<link>http://www.packtpub.com/news/master-
the-advanced-features-of-cryengine-with-
packts-new-book-and-ebook ?
utm_medium=rss</link>
<guid>http://www.packtpub.com/news/master-
the-advanced-features-of-cryengine-with-
packts-new-book-and-ebook </guid>
<pubDate>Wed, 28 May 2014 11:24:28
+0100</pubDate>
</item>
<item>
  <title>Learn cluster management and bulk
loading techniques to improve performance in
Vertica using Packt's new book and eBook</
title>
<description>About the Author:Rishabh
AgrawalRishabh Agrawal is a  senior database
research engineer and consultant at Impetus
India. He  has working knowledge of more than
```

The XML refresher

Extensible Markup Language (**XML**) is a data markup language that sets a series of rules and hierarchy to a data group, which is stored as a static file. Typically, servers update these XML files on the Web periodically to be reused as data sources. XML is really simple to pick up as it's similar to HTML. You can start with the document declaration in this case:

```
<?xml version="1.0" encoding="utf-8"?>
```

Next, a root node is set. A node is like an HTML tag (which is also called a node). You can tell it's a node by the brackets around the node's name. For example, here's a node named root:

```
<root></root>
```

Note that we close the node by creating a same-named node with a backslash. We can also add parameters to the node and assign a value, as shown in the following root node:

```
<root parameter="value"></root>
```

Data in XML is set through a hierarchy. To declare that hierarchy, we create another node and place that inside the parent node, as shown in the following code:

```
<root parameter="value">
    <subnode>Subnode's value</subnode>
</root>
```

In the preceding parent node, we created a subnode. Inside the subnode, we have an inner value called Subnode's value. Now, in programmatical terms, getting data from an XML data file is a process called parsing. With parsing, we specify where in the XML structure we would like to get a specific value; for instance, we can crawl the XML structure and get the inner contents like this:

```
/root/subnode
```

This is commonly referred to as **XPath** syntax, a cross-language way of going through an XML file. For more on XML and XPath, check out the full spec at: http://www.w3.org/TR/REC-xml/ and here http://www.w3.org/TR/xpath/ respectively.

RSS and the ATOM

Really simple syndication (RSS) is simply a variation of XML. RSS is a spec that defines specific nodes that are common for sending data. Typically, many blog feeds include an RSS option for users to pull down the latest information from those sites. Some of the nodes used in RSS include `rss`, `channel`, `item`, `title`, `description`, `pubDate`, `link`, and `GUID`.

Looking at our iPhone example in this chapter from the *Pulling data from the Web* section, we can see what a typical RSS structure entails. RSS feeds are usually easy to spot since the spec requires the root node to be named `rss` for it to be a true RSS file.

In some cases, some websites and services will use `.rss` rather than `.xml`; this is typically fine since most readers for RSS content will pull in the RSS data like an XML file, just like in the iPhone example.

Another form of XML is called **ATOM**. ATOM was another spec similar to RSS, but developed much later than RSS. Because of this, ATOM has more features than RSS: XML namespacing, specified content formats (video, or audio-specific URLs), support for internationalization, and multilanguage support, just to name a few.

ATOM does have a few different nodes compared to RSS; for instance, the root node to an RSS feed would be `<rss>`. ATOM's root starts with `<feed>`, so it's pretty easy to spot the difference. Another difference is that ATOM can also end in `.atom` or `.xml`.

For more on the RSS and ATOM spec, check out the following sites:

- `http://www.rssboard.org/rss-specification`
- `http://tools.ietf.org/html/rfc4287`

Understanding HTTP

All these samples from the RSS feed of the Packt Publishing website show one commonality that's used regardless of the technology coded in, and that is the method used to pull down these static files is through the **Hypertext Transfer Protocol (HTTP)**. HTTP is the foundation of Internet communication. It's a protocol with two distinct types of requests: a request for data or `GET` and a push of data called a `POST`.

Typically, when we download data using HTTP, we use the GET method of HTTP in order to pull down the data. The GET request will return a string or another data type if we mention a specific type. We can either use this value directly or save to a variable.

With a POST request, we are sending values to a service that handles any incoming values; say we created a new blog post's title and needed to add to a list of current titles, a common way of doing that is with URL parameters. A URL parameter is an existing URL but with a suffixed key-value pair.

The following is a mock example of a POST request with a URL parameter:

```
http://www.yourwebsite.com/blogtitles/?addtitle=Your%20New%20Title
```

If our service is set up correctly, it will scan the POST request for a key of `addtitle` and read the value, in this case: `Your New Title`. We may notice `%20` in our title for our request. This is an escape character that allows us to send a value with spaces; in this case, `%20` is a placehoder for a space in our value.

For the rest of this book, we will stick with GET requests, since we will only be reading data from the Web; however, this will give you an overview to get started in working in requests.

Using HTTP in Python

The RSS samples from the Packt Publishing website show a few commonalities we use in programming when working in HTTP; one is that we always account for the possibility of something potentially going wrong with a connection and we always close our request when finished. Here's an example on how the same RSS feed request is done in Python using a built-in library called `urllib2`:

```python
#!/usr/bin/env python
# -*- coding: utf-8 -*-

import urllib2

try:
    #Open the file via HTTP.
    response = urllib2.urlopen('http://www.packtpub.com/rss.xml')
    #Read the file to a variable we named 'xml'
```

```
    xml = response.read()
    #print to the console.
    print(xml)
    #Finally, close our open network.
    response.close()
except:
    #If we have an issue show a message and alert the user.
    print('Unable to connect to RSS...')
```

If we look in the following console output, we can see the XML contents just as we saw in our iOS code example:

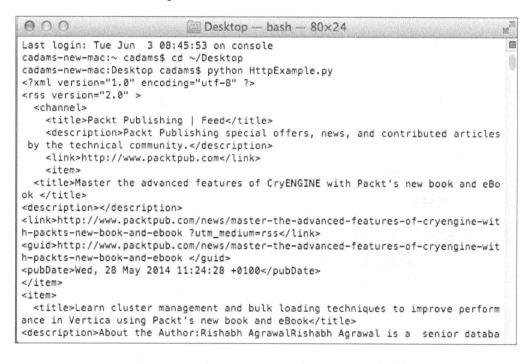

In the example, notice that we wrapped our HTTP request around a `try except` block. For those coming from another language, `except` can be considered the same as a `catch` statement. This allows us to detect if an error occurs, which might be an incorrect URL or lack of connectivity, for example, to programmatically set an alternate result to our Python script.

Parsing XML in Python with HTTP

With these examples including our Python version of the script, it's still returning a string of some sorts, which by itself isn't of much use to grab values from the full string. In order to grab specific strings and values from an XML pulled through HTTP, we need to parse it. Luckily, Python has a built-in object in the Python main library for this, called as `ElementTree`, which is a part of the XML library in Python.

Let's incorporate `ElementTree` into our example and see how that works:

```python
# -*- coding: utf-8 -*-

import urllib2
from xml.etree import ElementTree

try:
    #Open the file via HTTP.
    response = urllib2.urlopen('http://www.packtpub.com/rss.xml')

    tree = ElementTree.parse(response)
    root = tree.getroot()

    #Create an 'Element' group from our XPATH using findall.
    news_post_title = root.findall("channel//title")

    #Iterate in all our searched elements and print the inner text for
each.
    for title in news_post_title:
        print title.text

    #Finally, close our open network.
    response.close()
except Exception as e:
    #If we have an issue show a message and alert the user.
    print(e)
```

The following screenshot shows the results of our script:

```
● ○ ○                      🖵 Desktop — bash — 110×63
cadams-new-mac:~ cadams$ cd ~/Desktop
cadams-new-mac:Desktop cadams$ python HttpExample2.py
Packt Publishing | Feed
Create interactive web applications using WebRTC with Packt's new book and eBook
Speed up your game production workflow in GameMaker: Studio with Packt's new book and eBook
Metasploit Custom Modules and Meterpreter Scripting
Master game development using WebGL with Packt's new book and eBook
Understand and utilize the different capabilities of BizTalk Services using Packt&#039;s new book and eBook
Get hands-on with security vulnerabilities in Android applications and exploit them using Packt&#039;s new boo
k and eBook
Develop iOS applications with Xamarin using Packt's new book and eBook
Learn to optimize VMware environments using Packt's new book and eBook.
Configure ArcGIS for Server to achieve maximum performance and response time using Packt&#039;s new book and e
Book
Dive deep into Azure Mobile Services with a practical XAML-based case study using Packt&#039;s new book and eB
ook
Expand your knowledge of MicroStrategy using Packt&#039;s new book and eBook
Master the most popular and exciting framework for pen-testing with Packt's new video course
Learn to use Linux Mint like Professionals using Packt's new book and eBook
Learn penetration testing techniques using Packt's new book and eBook
Develop and deploy applications using the OSGi-based runtime container, Apache Karaf
Implement, configure, customize and manage Salesforce.com with Packt's new video
Create a reporting application from scratch using Packt&#039;s new book and eBook
Discover an ideal guide for getting the most out of MariaDB using Packt&#039;s new book and eBook
Learn to transfer JavaScript skills to server side programming using Packt new book and eBook
Get to grips with the exciting features and contents of PostGIS using Packt&#039;s new book and eBook!
Learn the advanced features of OpenERP using Packt's new book and eBook
Use machine learning and data-based methods to build intelligent applications using Packt&#039;s new book and
eBook
Master the configuration of JBoss EAP and become a well-rounded JBoss administrator with Packt's new video cou
rse
Configure and publish a Node package with Packt's new video course
Maximize the functionality and impact of reports created with SQL Server Reporting Services using Packt's new
video course
Maximize the functionality and impact of reports created with SQL Server Reporting Services using Packt's new
video course
Get to grips with flat design using Packt's new book and eBook
Get a grip of the power of SDL Trados Studio 2014 quickly and painlessly through Packt's new book and eBook
Learn over 70 recipes to design a virtual data center for performance, availability, manageability, and recove
rability with Packt&#039;s new book and eBook.
Master how to utilize Backbone Marionette using Packt&#039;s new book and eBook
Get to grips with designing Jade-based projects using Packt&#039;s new book and eBook
Master the advanced features of CryENGINE with Packt's new book and eBook
Learn cluster management and bulk loading techniques to improve performance in Vertica using Packt's new book
and eBook
Learn how to use PHPUnit to write and test code using Packt's new book and eBook
Build complex projects using the Arduino Yún with Packt&#039;s riveting new book and eBook
Master how to design and print 3D models with Packt&#039;s riveting new book and eBook
Create beautifully responsive site layouts using LESS with Packt's new book and eBook
Build a complete and secure XenDesktop 7 site using Packt's new book and eBook
Setting Up for Photoreal Rendering
Ruby and Metasploit Modules
Interacting with Data for Dashboards
Building a Private App
Working with the sharing plugin
3D Websites
Deploy your prototypes on devices and in users' hands using Axure 7 with Packt's new book and eBook.
Learn about cloud computing with Heroku using Packt's new book and eBook
Gain a deep and practical understanding of RabbitMQ with Packt's new book and eBook
Develop and customize your very own game quickly and easily in UDK using Packt's new video course
Design a road in Civil 3D using Packt's new video course
Create RESTful services with the ASP.NET web API using Packt's new video course
cadams-new-mac:Desktop cadams$ ▮
```

As we can see, our output shows each title for each blog post. Notice how we used `channel//item` for our `findall()` method. This is using XPath, which allows us to write in a shorthand manner on how to iterate an XML structure. It works like this; let's use the `http://www.packtpub.com` feed as an example. We have a root, followed by channel, then a series of title elements.

The `findall()` method found each element and saved them as an `Element` type specific to the XML library `ElementTree` uses in Python, and saved each of those into an array. We can then use a `for in` loop to iterate each one and print the inner text using the text `property` specific to the `Element` type.

You may notice in the recent example that I changed `except` with a bit of extra code and added `Exception as e`. This allows us to help debug issues and print them to a console or display a more in-depth feedback to the user. An `Exception` allows for generic alerts that the Python libraries have built-in warnings and errors to be printed back either through a console or handled with the code. They also have more specific exceptions we can use such as `IOException`, which is specific for working with file reading and writing.

About JSON

Now, another data type that's becoming more and more common when working with web data is **JSON**. JSON is an acronym for JavaScript Object Notation, and as the name implies, is indeed true JavaScript. It has become popular in recent years with the rise of mobile apps, and **Rich Internet Applications (RIA)**.

JSON is great for JavaScript developers; it's easier to work with when working in HTML content, compared to XML. Because of this, JSON is becoming a more common data type for web and mobile application development.

Parsing JSON in Python with HTTP

To parse JSON data in Python is a pretty similar process; however, in this case, our `ElementTree` library isn't needed, since that only works with XML. We need a library designed to parse JSON using Python. Luckily, the Python library creators already have a library for us, simply called `json`.

Let's build an example similar to our XML code using the `json` import; of course, we need to use a different data source since we won't be working in XML. One thing we may note is that there aren't many public JSON feeds to use, many of which require using a code that gives a developer permission to generate a JSON feed through a developer API, such as Twitter's JSON API. To avoid this, we will use a sample URL from Google's Books API, which will show demo data of *Pride and Prejudice, Jane Austen*. We can view the JSON (or download the file), by typing in the following URL:

```
https://www.googleapis.com/books/v1/volumes/s1gVAAAAYAAJ
```

 Notice the API uses HTTPS, many JSON APIs are moving to secure methods of transmitting data, so be sure to include the secure in HTTP, with HTTPS.

Let's take a look at the JSON output:

```
{
  "kind": "books#volume",
  "id": "s1gVAAAAYAAJ",
  "etag": "yMBMZ85ENrc",
  "selfLink": "https://www.googleapis.com/books/v1/volumes/
s1gVAAAAYAAJ",
  "volumeInfo": {
   "title": "Pride and Prejudice",
   "authors": [
    "Jane Austen"
   ],
   "publisher": "C. Scribner's Sons",
   "publishedDate": "1918",
   "description": "Austen's most celebrated novel tells the story of
Elizabeth Bennet, a bright, lively young woman with four sisters, and
a mother determined to marry them to wealthy men. At a party near the
Bennets' home in the English countryside, Elizabeth meets the wealthy,
proud Fitzwilliam Darcy. Elizabeth initially finds Darcy haughty and
intolerable, but circumstances continue to unite the pair. Mr. Darcy
finds himself captivated by Elizabeth's wit and candor, while her
reservations about his character slowly vanish. The story is as much
a social critique as it is a love story, and the prose crackles with
Austen's wry wit.",
   "readingModes": {
    "text": true,
    "image": true
   },
   "pageCount": 401,
   "printedPageCount": 448,
```

```
  "dimensions": {
   "height": "18.00 cm"
  },
  "printType": "BOOK",
  "averageRating": 4.0,
  "ratingsCount": 433,
  "contentVersion": "1.1.5.0.full.3",
  "imageLinks": {
   "smallThumbnail": "http://bks8.books.google.com/books?id=
s1gVAAAAYAAJ&printsec=frontcover&img=1&zoom=5&edge=curl&imgtk=
AFLRE73F8btNqKpVjGX6q7V3XS77QA2PftQUxcEbU3T3njKNxezDql_KgVko
fGxCPD3zG1yq39u0XI8s4wjrqFahrWQ-5Epbwfzfkoahl12bMQih5szba
Ow&source=gbs_api",
   "thumbnail": "http://bks8.books.google.com/books?id=s1
gVAAAAYAAJ&printsec=frontcover&img=1&zoom=1&
edge=curl&imgtk=AFLRE70tVS8zpcFltWh_7K_5Nh8BYugm2RgBS
Lg4vr9tKRaZAYoAs64RK9aqfLRECSJq7ATs_j38JRI3D4P48-2g_k4-
EY8CRNVReZguZFMk1zaXlzhMNCw&source=gbs_api",
   "small": "http://bks8.books.google.com/books?id=s1gVAAAAYAAJ
&printsec=frontcover&img=1&zoom=2&edge=curl&imgtk=AFLRE71qcidjIs
37x0jN2dGPstn6u2pgeXGWZpS1ajrGgkGCbed356114HPD5DNxcR5XfJtvU5DKy
5odwGgkrwY19gC9fo3y-GM74ZIR2Dc-BqxoDuUANHg&source=gbs_api",
   "medium": "http://bks8.books.google.com/books?id=s1gVAAAAYA
AJ&printsec=frontcover&img=1&zoom=3&edge=curl&imgtk=AFLRE73hIRCi
GRbfTb0uNIIXKW4vjrqAnDBSks_ne7_wHx3STluyMa0fsPVptBRW4yNxNKOJWjA4
Od5GIbEKytZAR3Nmw_XTmaqjA9CazeaRofqFskVjZP0&source=gbs_api",
   "large": "http://bks8.books.google.com/books?id=s1gVAAAAYAAJ
&printsec=frontcover&img=1&zoom=4&edge=curl&imgtk=AFLRE73mlnr
Dv-rFsL-n2AEKcOODZmtHDHH0QN56oG5wZsy9XdUgXNnJ_SmZ0sHGOxUv4sWK6
GnMRjQm2eEwnxIV4dcF9eBhghMcsx-S2DdZoqgopJHk6Ts&source=gbs_api",
   "extraLarge": "http://bks8.books.google.com/books?id=s1gVAAAA
YAAJ&printsec=frontcover&img=1&zoom=6&edge=curl&imgtk=AFLRE73KIX
HChsznTbrXnXDGVs3SHtYp18tGncDPX_7GH0gd7sq7SA03aoBR0mDC4-euzb4UCI
DiDNLYZUBJwMJxVX_cKG5OAraACPLa2QLDcfVkc1pcbC0&source=gbs_api"
  },
  "language": "en",
  "previewLink": "http://books.google.com/books?id=s1gVAAAAYAAJ&hl=&so
urce=gbs_api",
  "infoLink": "http://books.google.com/books?id=s1gVAAAAYAAJ&hl=&sour
ce=gbs_api",
  "canonicalVolumeLink": "http://books.google.com/books/about/Pride_
and_Prejudice.html?hl=&id=s1gVAAAAYAAJ"
  },
```

```
 "layerInfo": {
  "layers": [
   {
    "layerId": "geo",
    "volumeAnnotationsVersion": "6"
   }
  ]
 },
 "saleInfo": {
  "country": "US",
  "saleability": "FREE",
  "isEbook": true,
  "buyLink": "http://books.google.com/books?id=s1gVAAAAYAAJ&hl=&buy=&s
ource=gbs_api"
 },
 "accessInfo": {
  "country": "US",
  "viewability": "ALL_PAGES",
  "embeddable": true,
  "publicDomain": true,
  "textToSpeechPermission": "ALLOWED",
  "epub": {
   "isAvailable": true,
   "downloadLink": "http://books.google.com/books/download/Pride_and_
Prejudice.epub?id=s1gVAAAAYAAJ&hl=&output=epub&source=gbs_api"
  },
  "pdf": {
   "isAvailable": true,
   "downloadLink": "http://books.google.com/books/download/Pride_and_
Prejudice.pdf?id=s1gVAAAAYAAJ&hl=&output=pdf&sig=ACfU3U3dQw5JDWdbVgk2V
RHyDjVMT4oIaA&source=gbs_api"
  },
  "webReaderLink": "http://books.google.com/books/reader?id=s1gVAAAAYA
AJ&hl=&printsec=frontcover&output=reader&source=gbs_api",
  "accessViewStatus": "FULL_PUBLIC_DOMAIN",
  "quoteSharingAllowed": false
 }
}
```

One downside to JSON is that it can be hard to read complex data. So, if we run across a complex JSON feed, we can visualize it using a JSON Visualizer. Visual Studio includes one with all its editions, and a web search will also show multiple online sites where you can paste JSON and an easy-to-understand data structure will be displayed. Here's an example using `http://jsonviewer.stack.hu/` loading our example JSON URL:

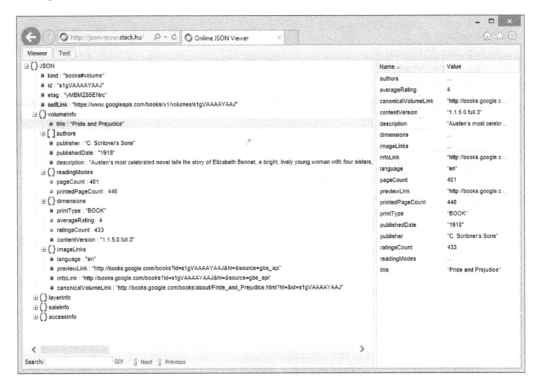

Next, let's reuse some of our existing Python code using our `urllib2` library to request our JSON feed, and then we will parse it with the Python's JSON library. Let's parse the `volumeInfo` node of the book by starting with the JSON (root) node that is followed by `volumeInfo` as the subnode. Here's our example from the XML section, reworked using JSON to parse all child elements:

```
# -*- coding: utf-8 -*-

import urllib2
import json
```

```python
try:
    #Set a URL variable.
    url = 'https://www.googleapis.com/books/v1/volumes/s1gVAAAAYAAJ'
    #Open the file via HTTP.
    response = urllib2.urlopen(url)

    #Read the request as one string.
    bookdata = response.read()

    #Convert the string to a JSON object in Python.
    data = json.loads(bookdata)

    for r in data ['volumeInfo']:
        print r

    #Close our response.
    response.close()

except:
    #If we have an issue show a message and alert the user.
    print('Unable to connect to JSON API...')
```

Here's our output. It should match the child nodes of volumeInfo, which it does in the output screen, as shown in the following screenshot:

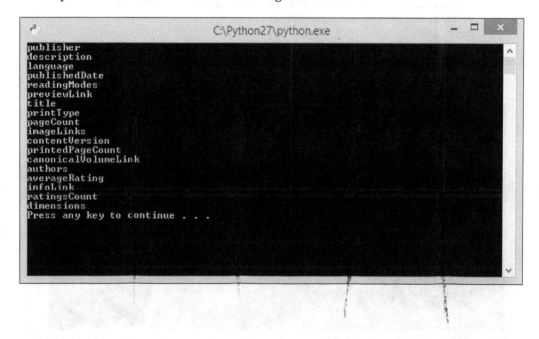

Well done! Now, let's grab the value for `title`. Look at the following example and notice we have two brackets: one for `volumeInfo` and another for `title`. This is similar to navigating our XML hierarchy:

```python
# -*- coding: utf-8 -*-

import urllib2
import json

try:
    #Set a URL variable.
    url = 'https://www.googleapis.com/books/v1/volumes/s1gVAAAAYAAJ'

    #Open the file via HTTP.
    response = urllib2.urlopen(url)

    #Read the request as one string.
    bookdata = response.read()

    #Convert the string to a JSON object in Python.
    data = json.loads(bookdata)

    print data['volumeInfo']['title']

    #Close our response.
    response.close()

except Exception as e:
    #If we have an issue show a message and alert the user.
    #'Unable to connect to JSON API...'
    print(e)
```

The following screenshot shows the results of our script:

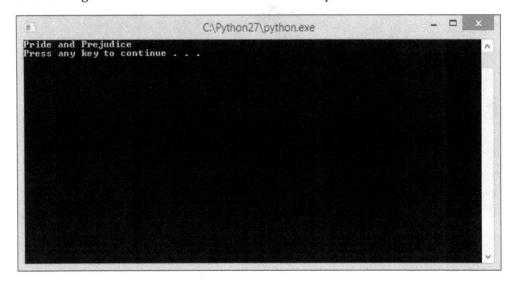

As you can see in the preceding screenshot, we return one line with `Pride and Prejudice` parsed from our JSON data.

About JSONP

JSONP, or JSON with Padding, is actually JSON but it is set up differently compared to traditional JSON files. JSONP is a workaround for web cross-browser scripting. Some web services can serve up JSONP rather than pure JSON JavaScript files. The issue with that is JSONP isn't compatible with many JSON Python-based parsers including one covered here, so you will want to avoid JSONP style JSON whenever possible.

So how can we spot JSONP files; do they have a different extension? No, it's simply a wrapper for JSON data; here's an example without JSONP:

```
/*
 *Regular JSON
 */
{ authorname: 'Chad Adams' }


The same example with JSONP:


/*
 * JSONP
 */
callback({ authorname: 'Chad Adams' });
```

Notice we wrapped our JSON data with a function wrapper, or a callback. Typically, this is what breaks in our parsers and is a giveaway that this is a JSONP-formatted JSON file. In JavaScript, we can even call it in code like this:

```
/*
 * Using JSONP in JavaScript
 */
callback = function (data) {
    alert(data.authorname);
};
```

JSONP with Python

We can get around a JSONP data source though, if we need to; it just requires a bit of work. We can use the `str.replace()` method in Python to strip out the callback before running the string through our JSON parser. If we were parsing our example JSONP file in our JSON parser example, the string would look something like this:

```
#Convert the string to a JSON object in Python.
data = json.loads(bookdata.replace('callback(', '').) .replace(')',
''))
```

Summary

In this chapter, we covered HTTP concepts and methodologies for pulling strings and data from the Web. We learned how to do that with Python using the `urllib2` library, and parsed XML data and JSON data. We discussed the differences between JSON and JSONP, and how to work around JSONP if needed.

In the next chapter, we will build a working simple application with the `pygal` library using dynamic web data.

7
Putting It All Together

Together we have been through a long process of learning Python data visualization development, handling data, and creating charts using the pygal library. Now it's time to put these skills to work. Our goal for this chapter is to use our knowledge to create a chart with dynamic data from the Web. In this chapter, we will cover the following topics:

- Import 2 months of RSS blog posts from the Web
- Format our RSS data for a new bar chart's dataset
- Build a simple bar chart to display blog posts for the past two months, passing in the number of posts
- Create a main application script to handle the execution and separate our code into modules, which we will import into our main script

Chart usage for a blog

We are going to start with the RSS feed from Packt Publishing and create a chart using data from the RSS feed. This chart will specifically comprise how many article posts are made in a month; at this point, we are familiar with parsing XML from a location found on the Web using HTTP. Then, we are going to create our own dataset from this feed.

To accomplish this, we will need to perform the following tasks:

- Find out how many posts are made in a given month
- Filter the count of posts for each month
- Finally, generate a chart based on this data for both months

Like any programming task, the key to success in both ease of writing and code maintainability, is breaking up the tasks required to accomplish the job. For this, we will break up this task into Python modules.

Getting our data in order

Our first task is to pull the RSS feed from the Packt Publishing website into our Python code. For this, we can reuse our Python HTTP and XML parser example from *Chapter 6, Importing Dynamic Data*, but instead of grabbing the titles for each `title` node, we will grab the date from `pubDate`. The `pubDate` object is an RSS standard convention to indicate the date and time in an XML-based RSS feed.

Let's modify our code from *Chapter 6, Importing Dynamic Data*, and grab the `pubDate` object. We will create a new Python script file and call it `LoadRssFeed.py`. Then, we will use this code in our editor of choice:

```python
#!/usr/bin/env python
# -*- coding: utf-8 -*-

import urllib2
from xml.etree import ElementTree

try:
    #Open the file via HTTP.
    response = urllib2.urlopen('http://www.packtpub.com/rss.xml')
    tree = ElementTree.parse(response)
    root = tree.getroot()

    #List of post dates.

    news_post_date = root.findall("channel//pubDate")

    '''Iterate in all our searched elements and print the inner text
for each.'''
    for date in news_post_date:
        print(date.text)

        #Finally, close our open network.
        response.close()

except Exception as e:
    #If we have an issue show a message and alert the user.
    print(e)
```

Notice rather than finding all titles, we are now finding pubDate using the XPath
path channel//pubDate. We also updated our date's list name to news_post_date.
This will help clarify our code. Let's run the code and see our results:

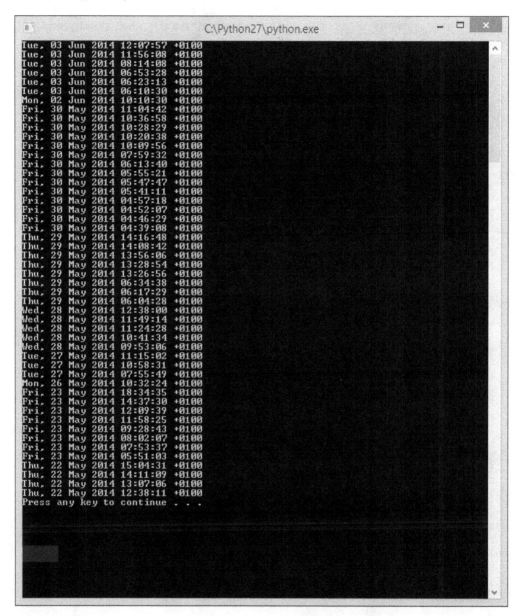

Looking good; we can tell we have a structured date and time format, and now we can filter by what is in the string, but let's dig a little more into this. Like in most languages, Python also has a `time` library that will allow for strings to be converted to `datetime` Python objects. How can we tell if these values aren't `date` objects already? Let's wrap our `print (date.text)` method in a `type` function to render the type of the object rather than the object's output, like this: `print type(date.text)`. Let's rerun the code and take a look at the results:

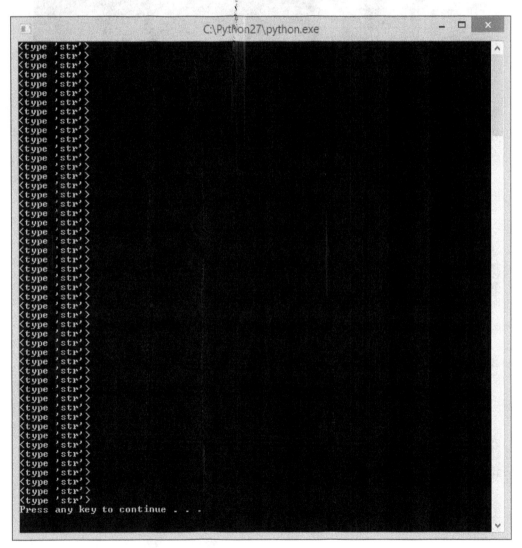

Converting date strings to dates

Before moving on, we need to convert any string we take in to useable types in Python, for instance, we pull in the publication date from our RSS feed. Wouldn't it be nice to have some already made functions to format or search our dates? Well, Python has a built-in type for this called `time`. Converting strings to `time` objects is pretty easy, but first, we need to add our import statement for `time` at the top of our code, for example, `import time`. Next, as our `pubDate` node isn't multiple strings that we easily set up to parse, let's split these up to an array using the `split()` method.

We will remove any commas in our string using the `replace()` method. We can even run this and our output window will show brackets around each `pubDate` with commas between each array item showing that we successfully split our single string to a string array.

Here we use a loop with a list of different time elements pulled from the RSS feed:

```
#!/usr/bin/env python
# -*- coding: utf-8 -*-

import urllib2
from xml.etree import ElementTree

try:
    #Open the file via HTTP.
    response = urllib2.urlopen('http://www.packtpub.com/rss.xml')
    tree = ElementTree.parse(response)
    root = tree.getroot()

    #List of post dates.
    news_post_date = root.findall("channel//pubDate")
    print(news_post_date)
    '''Iterate in all our searched elements and print the inner text
for each.'''
    for date in news_post_date:
        '''Create a variable striping out commas, and generating a new
array item for every space.'''
        datestr_array = date.text.replace(',', '').split(' ')
        '''Show each array in the Command Prompt(Terminal).'''
        print(datestr_array)

    #Finally, close our open network.
    response.close()

except Exception as e:
    '''If we have an issue show a message and alert the user.'''
    print(e)
```

Here, we can see as we loop through our our code, a list for each `time` object, month, day, year, time, and so on; this will help up grab specific time values in relation to our RSS feed we've parsed:

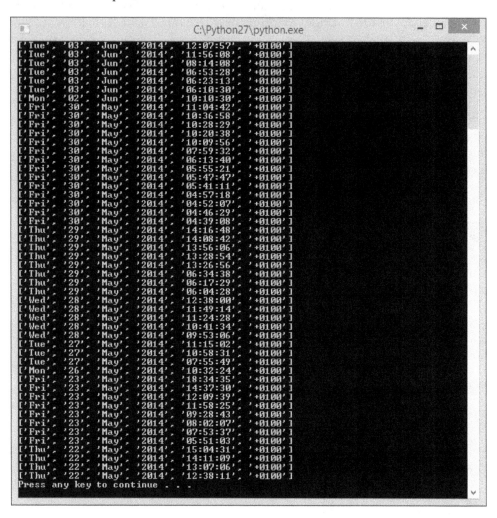

Using strptime

The `strptime()` method or strip time is a method found in the `time` module, and it allows us to create a `date` variable using our string arrays. All we need to do is specify the year, month, day, and time in our `strptime()` method. Let's create a variable for our string array created in our `for` loop. Then, create a `date` type variable with our `strptime()` method formatting it with our string array.

Take a look at the following code and notice how we structured the `for` loop using `news_post_date` list to match up our string array to show our list of dates received from the RSS feed, which we parse into Python `time` objects with the `strptime()` method. Let's go ahead and add the following code and take a look at our results:

```python
#!/usr/bin/env python
# -*- coding: utf-8 -*-

import urllib2, time
from xml.etree import ElementTree

try:
    #Open the file via HTTP.
    response = urllib2.urlopen('http://www.packtpub.com/rss.xml')
    tree = ElementTree.parse(response)
    root = tree.getroot()

    #Array of post dates
    news_post_date = root.findall("channel//pubDate")

    #Iterate in all our searched elements and print the inner text for each.
    for date in news_post_date:
        '''Create a variable striping out commas, and generating a new array item for every space.'''
        datestr_array = date.text.replace(',', '').split(' ')
        '''Create a formatted string to match up with our strptime method.'''
        formatted_date = "{0} {1}, {2}, {3}".format(datestr_array[2], datestr_array[1], datestr_array[3], datestr_array[4])

        #Parse a time object from our string.
        blog_datetime = time.strptime(formatted_date, "%b %d, %Y, %H:%M:%S")

        print blog_datetime

    #Finally, close our open network.
    response.close()

except Exception as e:
    #If we have an issue show a message and alert the user.
    print(e)
```

As we can see, each loop through the RSS feed shows a `time.struct_time` object. The `struct_time` object allows us to specify which part of the `time` object we want to work with; let's print only the month to the console:

We can now do this easily by printing `blog_datetime.tm_mon`, which references the `tm_mon` named parameter from our `struct_time` method. For example, here we get the number of the month for each post like this:

```python
#!/usr/bin/env python
# -*- coding: utf-8 -*-

import urllib2
from xml.etree import ElementTree
import time

def get_all_rss_dates():

    '''Create a global array to our function to save our month
counts.'''
    month_count = []

    try:
        #Open the file via HTTP.
        response = urllib2.urlopen('http://www.packtpub.com/rss.xml')
        tree = ElementTree.parse(response)
        root = tree.getroot()

        #Array of post dates.
        news_post_date = root.findall("channel//pubDate")

        '''Iterate in all our searched elements and print the inner
text for each.'''
        for date in news_post_date:
            '''Create a variable striping out commas, and generating a
new array item for every space.'''
            datestr_array = date.text.replace(',', '').split(' ')

            '''Create a formatted string to match up with our strptime
method.'''
            formatted_date = "{0} {1}, {2}, {3}".format(datestr_
array[2], datestr_array[1], datestr_array[3], datestr_array[4])

            '''Parse a time object from our string.'''
            blog_datetime = time.strptime(formatted_date, "%b %d, %Y,
%H:%M:%S")

            '''Add this date's month to our count array'''
            month_count.append(blog_datetime.tm_mon)
```

```
        #Finally, close our open network.
        response.close()

    except Exception as e:
        '''If we have an issue show a message and alert the user.'''
        print(e)
    for mth in month_count:
        print(mth)


#Call our function.
get_all_rss_dates()
```

The following screenshot shows the results of our script:

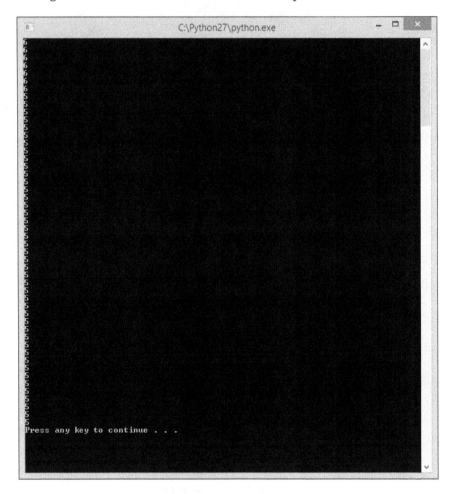

With this output, we can see the number 6, which indicates June, and the number 5, which indicates May. Great! We have now modified our code to consume data from the Web and display the same type data that we specify in our output. If you're curious about the string formats on `blog_datetime`, you can reference the string format index, which I've included in the following table. There is also a detailed list available at `https://docs.python.org/2/library/datetime.html#strftime-strptime-behavior`.

Placeholder	Description
%a	This is the abbreviated weekday name
%A	This is the weekday name without abbreviation
%b	This is the abbreviated month name
%B	This is the month name without abbreviation
%c	This is the preferred date and time representation
%C	This is the century of the date (2000 would return 20, 1900 would return 19)
%d	This shows the day of the month
%D	This is same as %m/%d/%y
%g	This is just like %G, but without the century
%G	This gives the four-digit year, such as 2014
%H	This shows the hour in the 24 hour format (00 to 23); most blogs use a 24-hour clock
%I	This gives the hour in the 12 hour format (01 to 12)
%j	Day of the year (001 to 366)
%m	Month (01 to 12)
%M	Minute
%p	Uses either a.m. or p.m.
%S	This displays the seconds of the date
%T	This gives the current time, which is equal to %H:%M:%S
%W	This is the week number of the current year
%w	Day of the week as a decimal, Sunday=0
%x	This gives the preferred date representation without the time
%X	This gives the preferred time representation without the date
%y	This only returns the last two digits of the year (for example, 2014 would return 14)

Placeholder	Description
%Y	This gives the year including the century (if the year is 2014, the output would be 2014)
%Z or %z	This gives the name of the time zone or abbreviation for the time zone (for example, Eastern standard time, or EST)

Saving the output as a counted array

With our data types in order, we want to count how many posts happen in a given month. For this, we will need to put each post into a grouped list we can use outside our `for` loop. We can do this by creating an empty array outside the `for` loop and add each `blog_datetime.tm_mon` object to our array.

Let's do this in the following code, but first, we will wrap this in a function as our code files are starting to get a bit large. If you remember back in *Chapter 2, Python Refresher*, we wrapped our large code blocks in functions so that we can reuse or clean up our code. We will wrap our code in the `get_all_rss_dates` name function and call it on the last line. Also, we will add the `month_count` array variable prior to our `try catch` ready-to-append values, which we did in our `for` loop, then print the `month_count` array variable. Let's take a look at what this renders:

```python
#!/usr/bin/env python
# -*- coding: utf-8 -*-

import urllib2
from xml.etree import ElementTree
import time

def get_all_rss_dates():
    #create a global array to our function to save our month counts.
    month_count = []

    try:
        #Open the file via HTTP.
        response = urllib2.urlopen('http://www.packtpub.com/rss.xml')
        tree = ElementTree.parse(response)
        root = tree.getroot()

        #Array of post dates.
        news_post_date = root.findall("channel//pubDate")

        '''Iterate in all our searched elements and print the inner
text for each.'''
        for date in news_post_date:
            '''Create a variable striping out commas, and generating a
new array item for every space.'''
            datestr_array = date.text.replace(',', '').split(' ')
```

```
            '''Create a formatted string to match up with our strptime
method.'''
            formatted_date = "{0} {1}, {2}, {3}".format(datestr_
array[2], datestr_array[1], datestr_array[3], datestr_array[4])

            '''Parse a time object from our string.'''
            blog_datetime = time.strptime(formatted_date, "%b %d, %Y,
%H:%M:%S")

            '''Add this dates month to our count array'''
            month_count.append(blog_datetime.tm_mon)

            '''Finally, close our open network.'''
            response.close()

    except Exception as e:
        '''If we have an issue show a message and alert the user.'''
        print(e)

    print month_count

#Call our function
get_all_rss_dates()
```

The following is a screenshot that shows our list of months and the numbers to correspond with the month. In this case, 5 is for the month of May and 6 is for the month of June (your numbers may change depending on the month):

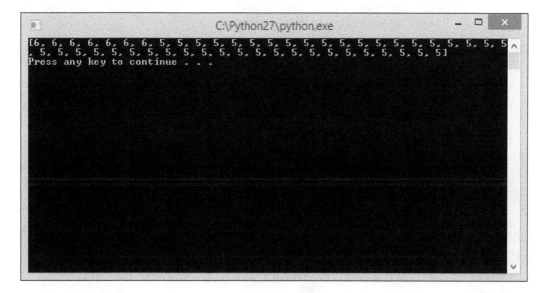

Counting the array

Now that our array is ready to work with, let's count the posts in both June and May. At the time of writing this book, we have seven posts in June and quite a lot in May.

Let's print out the number of blog posts the month of May has had on the Packt Publishing website news feed. To do this, we will use the count() method, which lets us search our array for a specific value. In this case, 5 is the value we are looking for:

```python
#!/usr/bin/env python
# -*- coding: utf-8 -*-

import urllib2
from xml.etree import ElementTree
import time

def get_all_rss_dates():

    '''create a global array to our function to save our month
counts.'''
    month_count = []

    try:
        #Open the file via HTTP.
        response = urllib2.urlopen('http://www.packtpub.com/rss.xml')
        tree = ElementTree.parse(response)
        root = tree.getroot()

        #Array of post dates.
        news_post_date = root.findall("channel//pubDate")

        '''Iterate in all our searched elements and print the inner
text for each. '''
        for date in news_post_date:
            '''Create a variable striping out commas, and generating a
new array item for every space.'''
            datestr_array = date.text.replace(',', '').split(' ')

            '''Create a formatted string to match up with our strptime
method.'''
            formatted_date = "{0} {1}, {2}, {3}".format(datestr_
array[2], datestr_array[1], datestr_array[3], datestr_array[4])
```

```
            '''Parse a time object from our string.'''
            blog_datetime = time.strptime(formatted_date, "%b %d, %Y,
%H:%M:%S")

            '''Add this date's month to our count array'''
            month_count.append(blog_datetime.tm_mon)

        '''Finally, close our open network. '''
        response.close()

    except Exception as e:
        '''If we have an issue show a message and alert the user. '''
        print(e)

    print month_count.count(5)

#Call our function
get_all_rss_dates()
```

As we can see in the following console, we get the number of posts that were written in the given month (in the screen and code, this is the month of May):

In our output window, we can see our result was 43 posts for the month of May in 2014. What if we change our count search to June, or rather, 6 in our code? Let's update our code and rerun:

Our output shows 7 as the total blog posts for the month of June. At this point, we've tested our code and now we have a working dataset to display for both May and June.

Python modules

Alright, so we've set up the data side of our chart, pulling data from the Web and parsing this data into useable objects in Python. We might think that it's now easy to plug these values into a pygal chart and call it a day, and in a way, this is correct; however, we want to be smart with our code.

Remember our discussion on how to wrap large chunks of Python code into functions; well, for a larger project, we would want to go even higher with modules; so, our first thought is: what is a module? Have we even used modules in the course of this book?

Yes, we have been using `time`, `pygal`, or `urllib2` any time we use an `import` statement in our code. That's a module, (sometimes called a library), and more interestingly, we can make our own modules, thereby allowing us to modularize our code.

Building the main method

In many programming languages, there exists a concept of a `main` function that is the very first function called in a program's execution. Let's create one here called `main_chartbuild` by simply creating the `main_chartbuild.py` file in our IDE.

Next, we want to remove the `get_all_rss_dates()` method call found during our initial testing in `LoadRssFeed` and then call our `get_all_rss_dates()` function's dates method using `import` in our `main_chartbuild.py` file. We will then reference our method but prefix it with our `import` name like this:

```python
#!/usr/bin/env python
# -*- coding: utf-8 -*-

import LoadRssFeed

#Call our 'LoadRssFeed' function.
LoadRssFeed.get_all_rss_dates()
```

If we rerun the script, we should see the same result as with our June post count, which is 7:

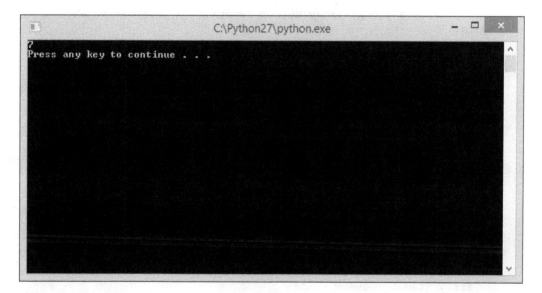

Modifying our RSS to return values

As we are using our `LoadRssFeed` as a library module now, we will want to modify the end result to return an array we can use in our `chart` module that we will build shortly. We will return two counts both in an array, one for May and one for June.

Also, we will remove the `print` statement as we understand that it is working properly. So, remove the `print` line at the end of the `LoadRssFeed`, `get_all_rss_dates` function and replace it with `return [month_count.count(5), month_count.count(6)]`. This will allow us to return a single object but keep two values for our chart. Here's the implementation of the file:

```python
#!/usr/bin/env python
# -*- coding: utf-8 -*-

import urllib2
from xml.etree import ElementTree
import time

def get_all_rss_dates():

    '''create a global array to our function to save our month
counts.'''
    month_count = []

    try:
        '''Open the file via HTTP.'''
        response = urllib2.urlopen('http://www.packtpub.com/rss.xml')
        tree = ElementTree.parse(response)
        root = tree.getroot()

        '''Array of post dates.'''
        news_post_date = root.findall("channel//pubDate")

        '''Iterate in all our searched elements and print the inner
text for each.'''
        for date in news_post_date:
            '''Create a variable striping out commas, and generating a
new array item for every space.'''
            datestr_array = date.text.replace(',', '').split(' ')

            '''Create a formatted string to match up with our strptime
method.'''
```

```
            formatted_date = "{0} {1}, {2}, {3}".format(datestr_
array[2], datestr_array[1], datestr_array[3], datestr_array[4])

            '''Parse a time object from our string.'''
            blog_datetime = time.strptime(formatted_date, "%b %d, %Y,
%H:%M:%S")

            '''Add this date's month to our count array'''
            month_count.append(blog_datetime.tm_mon)

        '''Finally, close our open network.'''
        response.close()

    except Exception as e:
        '''If we have an issue show a message and alert the user.'''
        print(e)

    '''Return two counts for both months.'''
    return [month_count.count(5), month_count.count(6)]
```

> Packt Publishing's website's RSS feed only accounts for the past two
> months of posts, so if you're reading this in October, for example, you
> would need to set the count to 10 for October and 9 for September for
> each `month_count` item.

Building our chart module

Next, let's create a new Python file to be our chart building library that uses pygal.
We will name this file `chart_build.py` and add this in our project root along with
our `LoadRssFeed.py` and `main_chartbuild.py` files.

Next, open the `chart_build.py` file and let's build a simple bar chart that shows
the number of posts for the months of May and June. Like our `LoadRssFeed`
module we built, we will wrap our chart code in a function with a parameter
called `dataarr`, indicating a data array. Before we add our data to our chart,
let's set up our chart configuration.

Building a portable configuration for our chart

In pygal, we typically create a chart, and inside it, we specify parameters to set settings for the chart and add our parameter values to the chart object that we call. The pygal library offers a way to modularize our configuration options.

This is helpful because in this example, we use only one chart but what if we had eight or twelve more charts to build? Having a portable configuration to set up the chart layout and theme can be very useful rather than rewriting the configuration each time.

Take a look at the following code. Here, I'm creating a Python class called ConfigChart, which has a parameter called Config that basically overrides the Config object in the chart we assign this to. Inside the class, I have a list of parameters that I can cleanly update and modify. Notice that I also import pygal, and using from pygal, I also import Config to work as a separate object:

```python
import pygal
from pygal import Config

'''Creating our own class with values to pass in as parameters to our
chart.'''
class ConfigChart(Config):
    show_legend = True
    human_readable = True
    fill = True
  '''explicit_size sets a fixed size to our width height
properties.'''
    explicit_size = True
    width = 860
    height = 640
    title= 'Posts per month on Packtpub.com'
    y_label = 'Posts'
    x_label = 'Month'
    y_title = 'Posts'
    x_title = 'Month'
    show_y_labels = True
    show_x_labels = True
    stroke = False
    tooltip_font_size = 42
    title_font_size = 24
  '''Always include an error message for any dynamic data.'''
    no_data_text = 'Unable to load data'
```

As you can see, I've added many of the values we discussed in *Chapter 5, Tweaking pygal,* and also ensured that our `no_data_text` parameter had a value in case of any connection issues. Also, as we want to render this in a browser, I've set the `width` and `height` as well as set a parameter called `explicit_size` to `True` to force the SVG output to a fixed size.

Setting up our chart for data

Now, let's finish setting up our chart to receive data in our `chart_build.py` file. Here, I've wrapped my pygal chart creation code in a function called `generate_chart` and added a parameter to handle our chart's data pulled from the RSS feed.

Here's the final code for the chart, including our `ConfigChart` class, applied to our chart object. Notice that for the `add()` methods for the chart, I simply added `dataarr` with an array index to specify the value for `May` and `June`, respectively:

```python
import pygal
from pygal import Config

'''Creating our own class with values to pass in as parameters to our
chart.'''
class ConfigChart(Config):
    show_legend = True
    human_readable = True
    fill = True
    '''explicit_size sets a fixed size to our width height
properties.'''
    explicit_size = True
    width = 860
    height = 640
    title= 'Posts per month on Packtpub.com'
    y_label = 'Posts'
    x_label = 'Month'
    y_title = 'Posts'
    x_title = 'Month'
    show_y_labels = True
    show_x_labels = True
    stroke = False
    tooltip_font_size = 42
    title_font_size = 24
    '''Always include an error message for any dynamic data.'''
    no_data_text = 'Unable to load data'
```

```
'''Generate chart based on imported array, (with 2 values)'''
def generate_chart(dataarr):

    '''Initialize the chart with our ConfigChart class.'''
    mychart = pygal.Bar(ConfigChart())

    '''Add data to the chart for May and June.'''
    mychart.add('May', dataarr[0])
    mychart.add('June', dataarr[1])

    '''Launch our web browser with our SVG, (we can also render to
file as well)'''
    mychart.render_in_browser()
```

Check our code in the `LoadRssFeed.py` file before running `main_chartbuild.py`.
We made one change here; we changed the `print` exception to `throw`, an exception if
we encounter a data connection issue in our `try/catch` block. If we were deploying
this application publically, we would add a UI error for a consumer rather than
an exception.

In this code, we've updated to return two values that we will pass into our chart:

```
#!/usr/bin/env python
# -*- coding: utf-8 -*-

import urllib2
from xml.etree import ElementTree
import time

def get_all_rss_dates():
    '''create a global array to our function to save our month
counts.'''
    month_count = []

    try:
        '''Open the file via HTTP. '''
        response = urllib2.urlopen('http://www.packtpub.com/rss.xml')
        tree = ElementTree.parse(response)
        root = tree.getroot()

        '''Array of post dates.'''
        news_post_date = root.findall("channel//pubDate")
```

```
        '''Iterate in all our searched elements and print the inner
text for each. '''
        for date in news_post_date:
            '''Create a variable striping out commas, and generating a
new array item for every space.'''
            datestr_array = date.text.replace(',', '').split(' ')

            '''Create a formatted string to match up with our strptime
method.'''
            formatted_date = "{0} {1}, {2}, {3}".format(datestr_
array[2], datestr_array[1], datestr_array[3], datestr_array[4])

            '''Parse a time object from our string.'''
            blog_datetime = time.strptime(formatted_date, "%b %d, %Y,
%H:%M:%S")

            '''Add this date's month to our count array'''
            month_count.append(blog_datetime.tm_mon)

        '''Finally, close our open network. '''
        response.close()

    except Exception as e:
        '''If we have an issue show a message and alert the user.'''
        throw

    #Return two counts for both months.
    return [month_count.count(5), month_count.count(6)]
```

Configuring our main function to pass data

One more task to do is set up our `main` function, which is our `main_chartbuild.py`, which is called when our script is executed. As our `LoadRssFeed` module returns an array that we pass into our chart, we will call the `generate_chart()` method from our `chart` module that we build and pass in the result, as shown in the following code:

```
#!/usr/bin/env python
# -*- coding: utf-8 -*-

import LoadRssFeed, chart_build

#Call our 'LoadRssFeed' function.
chart_build.generate_chart(LoadRssFeed.get_all_rss_dates())
```

Let's run our `main_chartbuild.py` file and take a look at the results:

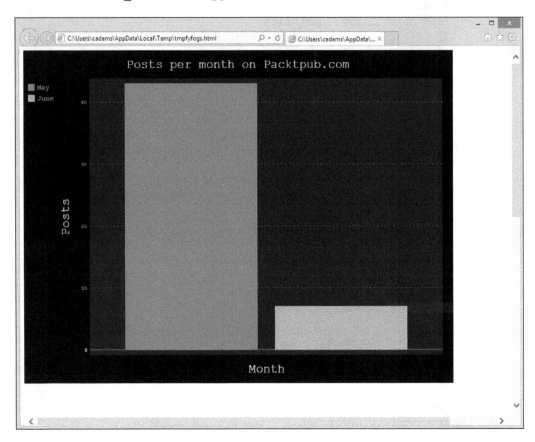

Project improvements

Success! We built a dynamic chart by pulling data from a web source and generated a chart with specific configurations that can be moved, updated, and replicated easily! Now, for our time together, this is a pretty simple example on a dynamic chart. Depending on the real-life situation, this script might auto-update every ten minutes, for example, on a chart-build server, or be called from another language with shell access that can trigger a Python script.

Also, think of the data and how it can create different kinds of charts. We can create arrays using our `LoadRssFeed` module we built together and pull how many posts a specific author has, or how many times a specific word shows up in a blog post's title. We have experienced working through a complex application in Python and taking live data on the web pulling into our chart to be displayed.

The following is the modified code that is independent of a month:

```
import pygal
from pygal import Config

'''Creating our own class with values to pass in as parameters to our
chart. '''
class ConfigChart(Config):
    show_legend = True
    human_readable = True
    fill = True
    #explicit_size sets a fixed size to our width height properties.
    explicit_size = True
    width = 860
    height = 640
    title= 'Posts per month on Packtpub.com'
    y_label = 'Posts'
    x_label = 'Month'
    y_title = 'Posts'
    x_title = 'Month'
    show_y_labels = True
    show_x_labels = True
    stroke = False
    tooltip_font_size = 42
    title_font_size = 24
    #Always include an error message for any dynamic data.
    no_data_text = 'Unable to load data'

'''Generate chart based on imported array, (with 2 values) '''
def generate_chart(dataarr):

    '''Initialize the chart with our ConfigChart class. '''
    mychart = pygal.Bar(ConfigChart())

    '''Add data to the chart for May and June. '''
    for data in dataarr:
        mychart.add(data[0], data[1])
    #mychart.add('June', dataarr[1])

    '''Launch our web browser with our SVG,
    (we can also render to file as well) '''
    mychart.render_in_browser()
```

```
if __name__ == '__main__':
    generate_chart([('May', 10), ('June', 20), ('July', 30)])
```

LoadRssFeed.py

```
import urllib2
from xml.etree import ElementTree
from collections import defaultdict

def get_all_rss_dates():

    month_count = defaultdict(int)

    try:
        #Open the file via HTTP.
        response = urllib2.urlopen('http://www.packtpub.com/rss.xml')
        tree = ElementTree.parse(response)
        root = tree.getroot()

        news_post_date = root.findall("channel//pubDate")

        #Iterate in all our searched elements and print the inner text
for each.
        for date in news_post_date:
            month_count[ date.text[8:11]] += 1

        response.close()

    except Exception as e:
        #If we have an issue show a message and alert the user.
        throw

    return list(month_count.items())

if __name__ == '__main__':
    print(get_all_rss_dates())
```

Summary

In this chapter, we put together a basic, yet real-life working dynamic chart application using the RSS data pulled dynamically from the Web using HTTP. We created a chart using the pygal library, then modified our chart using the pygal's Config class, and automatically launched the web browser to display the chart.

8
Further Resources

So we may ask, what now? What else is there to know? Well, quite a bit actually, as mentioned at the beginning back in *Chapter 1*, *Setting Up Your Development Environment*, and other chapters as well, this is an introduction to data visualizations using Python, but not the entirety.

Building dynamic charts in Python is a skillset that's very much in demand these days. The reason being is twofold; for one, Python is free and cross-platform allowing build servers to exist on a Linux server, a Microsoft IIS server; or a Mac server, you get the idea.

The other reason is that Python works very fast with processing data computations, specifically regarding medical, atmospheric, or even financial data to name a few. Depending on the types of data needing different styles of charts with different interactivity, we will need to use different charting libraries, which begs the question, what else is out there beyond pygal?

The matplotlib library

In the Python world of graphics and data charting, one of the most popular libraries out there is **matplotlib**. While the name may sound silly, `matplotlib` is simply put, a 2D and 3D plotting library that generates production quality, hardcopy graphics and charts. Now, the `matplotlib` library can be easy to work with early on, but it can get very complex quickly.

Remember back in *Chapter 2*, *Python Refresher*, we discussed creating our own graphics, and charts from scratch? Well, matplotlib allows us to not only build charts and graphs, but also draw graphics, widgets, and run animations both in 2D static images and 3D objects created within the framework. Check out the examples on the matplotlib website: `http://matplotlib.org/examples/index.html`.

Installing the matplotlib library

Remember back at the start of *Chapter 3, Getting Started with pygal*, pygal required the installation of lxml? Well, so does matplotlib, but with a different set of libraries, on Linux systems; matplotlib is easily installable through most Linux general Python package managers with all its required dependencies by using the following command, thus you don't require a Debian installer:

```
sudo apt-get install Python-matplotlib
```

 If you are using a Windows-based system, consider using a Mac or Linux-based system, since they require a bit of extra work to get matplotlib installed properly. If you only have access to Windows, consider installing a virtual machine with an OS such as Ubuntu.

The following screenshots shows the matplotlib **Downloads** page:

matplotlib's library download page

Now, if you're working in Windows or Mac-based OS, matplotlib recommends downloading a binary installer for matplotlib, for which the developers' created an exe installer for Windows machines, or dmg installer for Mac systems. This allows C imaging code to be installed properly to the machine, like `lxml` in *Chapter 1, Setting Up Your Development Environment*, for Window's systems. You can grab the installer for Windows and Mac here: `http://matplotlib.org/downloads.html`.

 For Mac users for matplotlib, the links at the time of writing this show 10.6 as the only installer; these will work on any Intel Mac, including 10.9 Mavericks.

If you do run into an issue with matplotlib on Linux systems, tarball installers for that platform can be found on that page as well; be sure to install the version that goes along with your Python's runtime.

One dependency is that matplotlib uses Numeric Python or NumPy to handle complex math, and is commonly used in basic chart creation, and/or for creating curves in data. Downloading this dependency is a bit easier through pip, by using the pip command shown in the following command. If you run into issues, check out installing the SciPy stack at `http://www.scipy.org/`, which also includes `maplotlib` along with extra plugins.

```
sudo pip install numpy
```

 For Windows users, NumPy does not include a 64-bit version. You will need a 32-bit version of Python 2.7 to run it.

Creating simple matplotlib charts

Most basic charts in matplotlib are fairly easy to build once your libraries and dependencies are installed. In the following code, we have a sample code with standard Python and Unicode declarations and we simply create a list numbers using a range of `0 - 541`, then we add values to our chart using a simple `for` loop, and save the file while also showing it in the matplotlib viewer:

```
#!/usr/bin/env Python
# -*- coding: utf-8 -*-

from matplotlib import pyplot
```

```
#Create a range from 0 - 541
X = range(0, 541)


#Set the values for Y by iterating thru X's range.
Y = [i*i for i in X]

'''Assign a range of values to the graph, the dash goes between each
value.'''
pyplot.plot(X, Y, '-')


#Set chart's labels and title
pyplot.title('Plotting x*x')
pyplot.xlabel('X Axis')
pyplot.ylabel('Y Axis')

#Save the chart as a PNG to our project directory.
pyplot.savefig('Simple.png')

#Show the chart in the Python runtime viewer.
pyplot.show()
```

The following screenshot shows the result of our script:

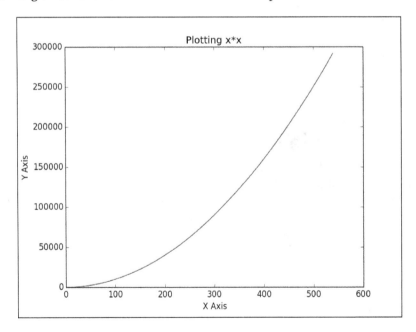

Notice here that our chart's `Simple.png` file that was created with the `savefig()` function is actually transparent. This is due to how matplotlib renders PNG charts. Now, if we look at the last line, `pyplot.show()`, this will tell `matplotlib` to display the following window showing the same chart we saved to our `Simple.png` file.

The following is our chart using Python's chart viewer supplied by matplotlib. You can manipulate the chart using the controls at the bottom-left:

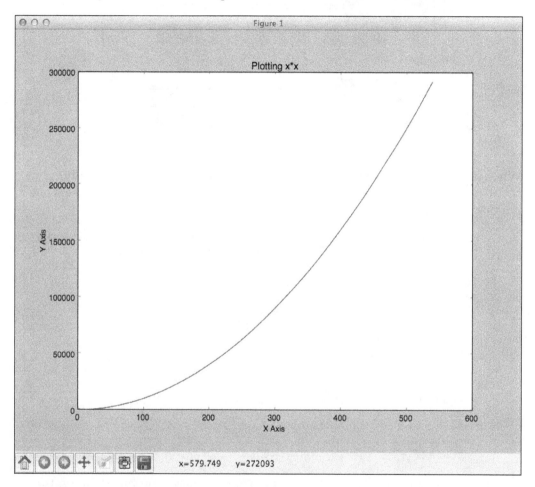

One of the controls that can be found next to the **save** button is the **Subplot Configuration Tool**. Clicking that opens a subset of controls to tweak the chart, as shown in the following screenshot:

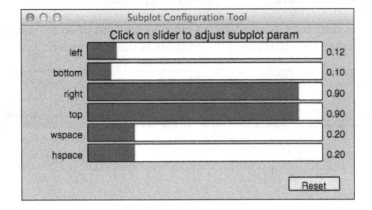

When satisfied with how your chart looks, you can save it with the **save** button. If you make a mistake, you can click on **reset** or click the **home** button on the main window's toolbar.

The `matplotlib` library includes many standard chart types as well as 3D-supported charts. Let's build a simple 3D chart. Take a look at the following code:

```
#!/usr/bin/env Python
# -*- coding: utf-8 -*-

from mpl_toolkits.mplot3d import Axes3D
import numpy as np
import matplotlib.pyplot as plt

fig = plt.figure()
ax = fig.gca(projection='3d')

#Create a curve on the z axis.
x = np.linspace(0, 1, 100)
y = np.sin(x * -1 * np.pi) / 2 + 0.5

ax.plot(x, y, zs=0, zdir='z', label='Our random sin curve, only for
z-axis')

'''Specify colors, and loop thru each and randomize the scatter dots,
and add them to the chart data.'''
colors = ('r', 'g', 'k', 'b')
for c in colors:
    x = np.random.sample(42)
    y = np.random.sample(42)
```

```
        ax.scatter(x, y, 1, zdir='x', c=c)

#Apply the legend.
ax.legend()

#Add the X, Y, and Z axis.
ax.set_xlim3d(0, 1)
ax.set_ylim3d(0, 1)
ax.set_zlim3d(0, 1)

#Show the chart.
plt.show()
```

For this chart, notice we are using `mpl_toolkits`, a module of `matplotlib`; this includes the `Axes3D` module. This allows us to draw 3D-based charts. Here we're going to draw a curve on the *z* axis, and randomly scatter multicolored dots on the *x* axis. Let's run the code and look at the results:

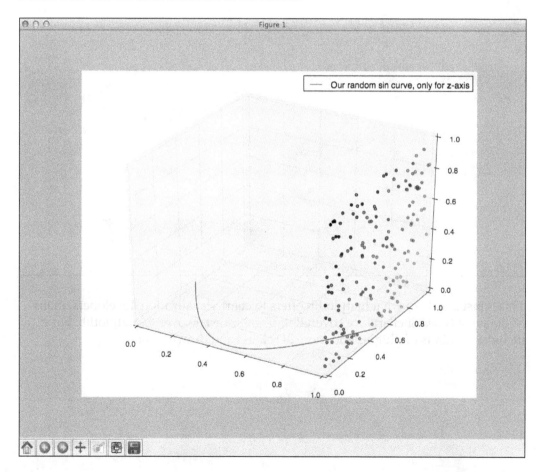

One great feature of 3D charts with `matplotlib` is that we can rotate 3D charts with a mouse, by dragging the mouse over the chart image; here's an example of updating the chart to get a better angle with the dots and the curve:

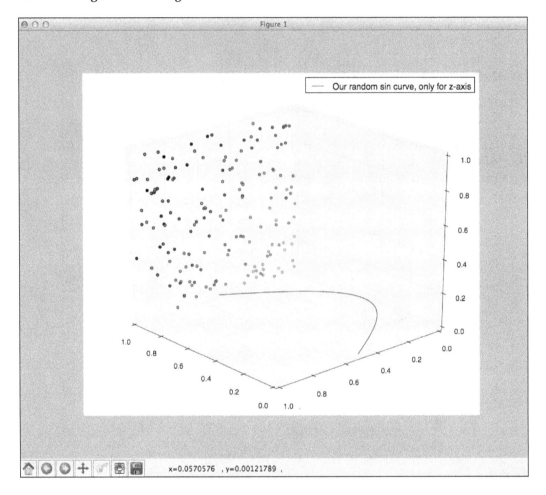

This is just a taste of what matplotlib offers to chart visualization developers, many of the same types of charts we covered in pygal translate over to matplotlib, but it includes all kinds of plugins and more 3D charts and drawing tools.

For more on this library, check out the matplotlib website. Considering its popularity, there are plenty of books on the topic to get you started with various entry points into the library.

Plotly

Plotly (`https://plot.ly/`) is a new charting library in the Python data visualization space. What separates Plotly from other charting Python libraries is that it is very business- and organization-oriented. Plotly is a company, unlike some other libraries on the Web. Python developers need to sign up on the website for a developer account to receive an API key to use in code, as shown in the following screenshot:

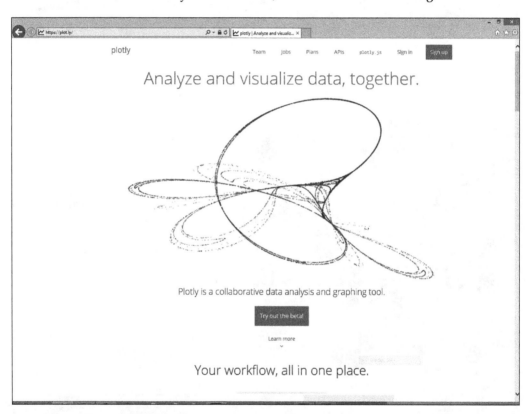

The concept of Plotly is simple. Charts are created in either an online tool hosted on Plotly's website, or by code; in our case, a Python library that integrates with Plotly's services, since Plotly hosts each saved chart, and it allows hosted charts to be shared. This is helpful in sharing data with non-technical users. For example, the following is a screenshot of a chart made in the Plotly editor that a user can share on the web:

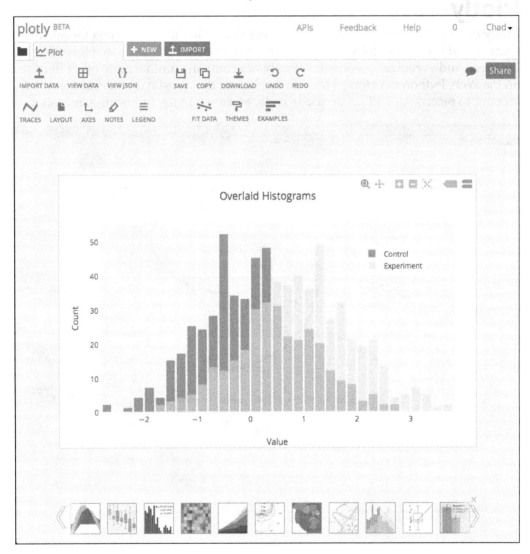

The advantage Plotly gives is that it's easy to share interactive charts. Plotly also has an online tool shown in the preceding screenshot, to create charts without any code, and upload data to display to an online shareable chart. Developers can also use Plotly on Chrome OS by using its Chrome app.

On the flip side, Plotly works well as a cloud-based library. It's important to know that Plotly's library requires Python 3 or higher; so before installing, we will need to download Python 3 from Python's website (http://www.python.org/). Before installing Plotly, you can also run Python 3 alongside 2 if required. Installation for Plotly with Python 3 is very easy as well. The `plotly` library can be installed easily using `pip`, as shown in the following code:

```
pip install plotly
```

Remember that Plotly requires Python 3 or higher to work. Otherwise, if pip is run in Python 2.7, some of the dependencies won't be installed. Now, once we've installed our library, we need to specify our login information for the API, this is specific to the login or OpenID used on the `https://plot.ly/` site. Be sure to include the login information requested; otherwise, any charts will result in a dialog similar to what is shown in the following screenshot:

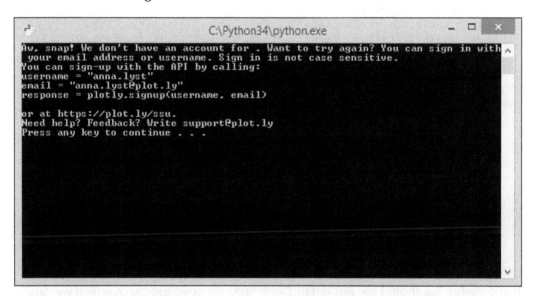

Fortunately, Plotly has a page where if you're logged in, it will generate a sample login object with user-specific information. We can find this at `https://plot.ly/Python/getting-started/`.

With that added, let's build a simple chart in Plotly. Here, we will import Plotly to our script and again as a module, all the chart types for us to use, and finally our information to use the API.

Here, we will build a simple line chart with some sample data. Copy the following code and run the script, keeping in mind a registered username and API key will be needed to run the script. In the following code sample, I've added placeholders in brackets to fill in:

```python
#!/usr/bin/env python
# -*- coding: utf-8 -*-

'''import Plotly, and the main plotly object as a variable.'''
import plotly;
import plotly.plotly as py

'''import all chart types.'''
from plotly.graph_objs import *

'''Set the username, APIKey, and streaming IDs as given on https://
plot.ly/python/getting-started/'''
plotly.tools.set_credentials_file(username='[username]', api_
key='[apikey]', stream_ids=['[streamingkey1]', '[streamingkey2]'])

'''Create a data-set for a Plotly scatter plot.'''
trace0 = Scatter(
    x=[5, 10, 15, 20],
    y=[20, 40, 35, 16]
)

'''Assign the chart's data to an array typed variable (in this case
trace0) to hold data.'''
data = Data([trace0])

'''Create a URL with the data loaded via the API, and open a web
browser to the chart on success.'''
unique_url = py.plot(data, filename = 'basic-line')
```

If successful, we should see our default web browser open the chart, which we can share easily via the social network icons in the left-hand side of our Plotly viewer on the Web. Notice that if we hover over the chart, we can get animations and data similar to pygal, but we can also zoom into the charts or select specific areas of the chart for more complex data.

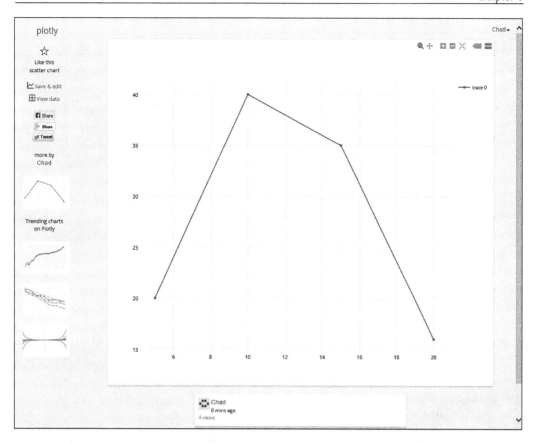

Well done! Let's build one more chart. This time it will be a scatter plot with two datasets. We will do a mock chart comparing NASCAR fans with Formula 1 fans sampled from Europe and the United States (keep in mind, this is just sample data).

In this chart, we will also incorporate some labels to better style the chart, and format the dots with our own styles. Again, we will need our API login and keys; placeholders have been set up in this code sample:

```python
#!/usr/bin/env python
# -*- coding: utf-8 -*-

'''import Plotly, and the main plotly object as a variable.'''
import plotly;
import plotly.plotly as py

'''import all chart types.'''
```

```
from plotly.graph_objs import *

'''Set the username, APIKey, and streaming IDs as given on https://
plot.ly/python/getting-started/'''

plotly.tools.set_credentials_file(username='[username]', api_
key='[apikey]', stream_ids=['[streamingkey1]', '[streamingkey2]'])

'''Create a data-set for a scatter plot.'''
trace0 = Scatter(
    #Create an array for each value.
    x=[27984, 9789],
    y=[34, 27],
    text=['Formula 1 Fans', 'Nascar Fans'],
    name='European automotive fans',
    mode='markers',
    marker=Marker(
        line=Line(
            color='rgb(124, 78, 42)',
            width=0
        ),
        size=48,
        color='rgb(124, 78, 42)'
    )
)

trace1 = Scatter(
    #Create an array for each value.
    x=[10117, 340159],
    y=[38, 31],
    text=['Formula 1 Fans', 'Nascar Fans'],
    name='North America automotive fans',
    mode='markers',
    marker=Marker(
        line=Line(
            color='rgb(114, 124, 195)',
            width=0
        ),
        size=48,
        color='rgb(114, 124, 195)'
    )
)

'''Set chart's titles, labels, and values.'''
layout = Layout(
    title='Fan comparisons of automotive sports in the United States
and Europe',
    xaxis=XAxis(
        title='Amount of fans',
        showgrid=True,
```

```
            zeroline=False
        ),
    yaxis=YAxis(
            title='Average age of fans sampled',
            showline=True
        )
    )

'''Assign the data to an array typed variable to hold data.'''
data = Data([trace0, trace1])

'''Add full chart labels to the chart.'''
fig = Figure(data=data, layout=layout)

'''Create a URL with the data loaded via the API, pass the data to the
figure which is passed here, and then open a web browser to the chart
on success.'''
unique_url = py.plot(fig, filename = 'line-style')
```

The following screenshot shows the result of our script:

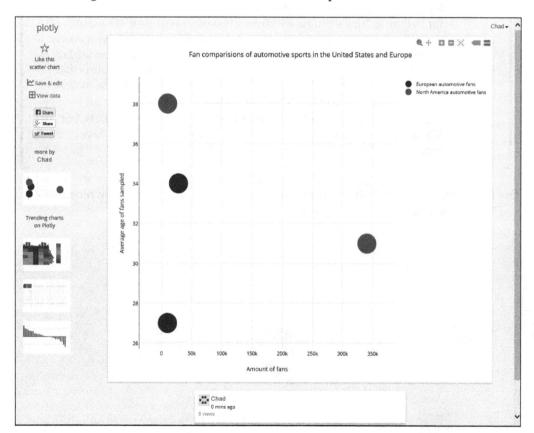

So as we can see, Plotly is very easy to work with, and with our pygal background, this will work well for any future projects. For info on the Plotly API with Python, check out the developer site at `https://plot.ly/Python/`.

Pyvot

Pyvot (`http://pytools.codeplex.com/wikipage?title=Pyvot`) is a Python data to Microsoft Excel converter, which is a very handy tool for exporting chart data or general Python values to Excel. It can be installed using `pip` like this:

```
pip install Pyvot
```

You can also install it with `easy_install`:

```
easy_install Pyvot
```

One thing to be noted is that at the end of writing this book, Pyvot is no longer maintained by the author, and is mostly being used for tech demos for Python in Visual Studio by Microsoft staff or Microsoft MVPs, so we will refrain from posting sample code in this book. Should you need documentation on Pyvot's CodePlex site, `http://pytools.codeplex.com/wikipage?title=Pyvot` is helpful. Another thing to note is that Pyvot can be commonly found in some Python charting projects, mainly due to the tight integration with Visual Studio and Excel.

The library itself still works very well with Python 2 and 3 projects, but if a maintained library is desired, check out: **PyXLL** (`https://www.pyxll.com/`) or **DataNitro** (`https://datanitro.com/`).

The following screenshot shows the CodePlex site for Pyvot with a download link and video documentation walkthrough:

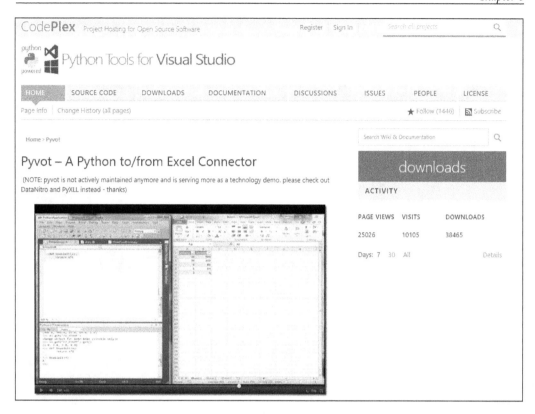

Summary

In this chapter, we wrapped things up with an overview and basic usage of both `matplotlib` and Plotly. We touched upon exporting data by using libraries such as Pyvot, PyXLL, and DataNitro.

One takeaway from this book is that the choices for data visualization are huge in the Python language. My advice for new and current Python developers is to find a library that works well for your needs and the goals of your projects. For this book, we covered the `pygal` library due to its simplicity and its easy to use documentation, as mentioned in *Chapter 3, Getting Started with pygal*. Now try some of these other libraries mentioned in this chapter and see what data visualization library works best for you.

References and Resources

The Python community offers quite a few resources and tools when working with data visualization libraries, as well as community help. Here is a list of sites for further reading, including the libraries covered in this book.

Links for help and support

The following are links for help and support:

- Kozea, creators of pygal, and a general open source discussion board can be found at `http://community.kozea.fr`
- Stack overflow for general Python questions can be found at `http://stackoverflow.com/questions/tagged/Python`
- Stack overflow questions for data visualizations with Python can be found at `http://stackoverflow.com/questions/tagged/data-visualization+Python`
- Snipplr for Python code (great for Python code snippets) can be found at `http://snipplr.com/all/language/Python`

Charting libraries

The following are links for different charting libraries:

- matplotlib can be found at `http://matplotlib.org`
- pygal can be found at `http://pygal.org`
- Plotly can be found at `https://plot.ly`
- PyChart can be found at `http://home.gna.org/pychart/`
- iGraph: can be found at `http://igraph.org/redirect.html`
- NetworkX can be found at `http://networkx.github.io`

- Graphviz can be found at `http://www.graphviz.org/Gallery.php`
- pygooglechart (a Python wrapper for Google charts) can be found at `https://github.com/gak/pygooglechart`

Editors and IDEs for Python

The following are links for different editors and IDEs for Python:

- Python tools for Visual Studio (used primarily with this book, and works well with pygal) can be found at `http://pytools.codeplex.com`
- PyDev for Eclipse can be found at `http://pydev.org`
- CodeRunner for Mac (a nice editor for running quick Python scripts and works well with matplotlib projects) can be found at `http://krillapps.com/coderunner/`
- Sublime Text (a great, lightweight editor for cross-platform editing) can be found at `http://www.sublimetext.com`
- PyCharm (a full IDE alternative to PyDev and Visual Studio) can be found at `http://www.jetbrains.com/pycharm/`

Other libraries and Python alternative shells

The following are links for other libraries and Python alternative shells:

- Anaconda can be found at `https://store.continuum.io/cshop/anaconda/`
- Canopy can be found at `https://www.enthought.com/products/canopy/`
- Python Imaging Library (PIL), a common imaging library in Python, can be found at `http://www.Pythonware.com/products/pil/`
- IPython (a feature rich shell, commonly used for matplotlib projects) can be found at `http://iPython.org`
- IronPython (Python plus access to the .NET framework and WPF visualization tools) can be found at `http://ironPython.net`
- Jython (Python with Java access) can be found at `http://www.jython.org`
- Pyvot can be found at `http://pytools.codeplex.com/wikipage?title=Pyvot`
- PyXLL can be found at `https://www.pyxll.com/`
- DataNitro can be found at `https://datanitro.com/`

Index

A

Anaconda
  URL 190
array
  counting 158-160
ATOM
  about 131
  URL, for specification 131

B

bar chart
  about 71
  building 71
basics, Python
  about 35-40
  image, generating 45-48
  input 42-45
  libraries, importing 40-42
  modules, importing 40-42
  output 42-45
blog
  chart, used for 145
box plots 89-91

C

Canopy
  URL 190
chart
  portable configuration,
      building for 164, 165
  setting up, for data 165, 166
  used, for blog 145
chart module
  building 163

chart title settings 120-122
chart usage, for blog
  data, rearranging 146-148
  date strings, converting to dates 149
  output saving, as counted array 156-160
  strptime, using 150-154
CodePlex site
  URL 186
CodeRunner, for Mac
  URL 190
counted array
  creating 156, 157
country chart 105-107
craft_type array 98

D

data
  chart, setting up for 165, 166
  extracting, from Web 127-129
  passing, via main function
      configuration 167
  rearranging 146-148
DataNitro
  URL 186, 190
dataset
  creating 145
dates
  date strings, converting to 149
date strings
  converting, to dates 149
datetime library 78
DateY charts
  about 78
  building 78-82
dot_chart class 91
dot charts 91-94

E

easy_install 7, 48
Eclipse Classic
  URL 33
Eclipse Kepler
  URL 28
editors, Python
  URL 190
Extensible Markup Language. *See* XML

F

findall() method 136
funnel charts
  about 94, 95
  advantage 94

G

gauge charts 96-98
Graphviz
  URL 190

H

horizontal bar charts 73
HTTP (Hypertext Transfer Protocol)
  about 131, 132
  JSON, parsing in Python 136-143
  using, in Python 132, 133
  XML, parsing in Python 134-136

I

IDEs, Python
  URL 190
iGraph
  URL 189
installation, PIL 46
installation, Python
  in Windows 15-19
installer, Mac
  URL 173
installer, Windows
  URL 173
IPython
  URL 190

IronPython

about 23
URL 23, 190

J

JSON
  about 136
  parsing, in Python 136-143
  URL 137
JSONP (JSON with Padding)
  about 143
  using, with Python 144
Jython
  URL 190

K

Kozea
  URL 189

L

label_font_size parameter 117
label settings 116-120
legend_at_bottom parameter 109, 110
legend box
  formatting, legend_box_size parameter
    used 111-116
legend_box_size parameter
  used, for formatting legend box 111-116
legend settings 111
line.add() statement 69
line chart
  building 67-69
lxml library 16, 64

M

Mac OS X
  Python, setting up on 25-30
main function
  configuring, for passing data 167
matplotlib
  URL 189
matplotlib charts
  creating 173-178

matplotlib library
  about 171
  download page 173
  installing 172
  matplotlib charts, creating 173-178
matplotlib website
  URL 171

N

Neon 124
NetworkX
  URL 189
no data
  displaying 123
no_data_text parameter 123

P

parameters
  about 108, 109
  legend_at_bottom parameter 109, 110
  legend box formatting, legend_box_size
      parameter used 111-116
  legend settings 111
pie charts
  about 85, 86
  stacked pie charts 86, 87
Pie() function 86
PIL
  about 45
  installing 46
  URL 190
pip
  about 7
  used, for installing pygal 64, 65
Plotly
  about 179-186
  advantage 181
  URL 179, 189
Plotly API
  URL 186
portable configuration
  building, for chart 164, 165
project improvements 168
pubDate object 146

PyCharm
  URL 190
PyChart
  URL 189
PyDev, Eclipse
  URL 190
pygal
  about 61-64
  DateY charts 78
  features 61, 62
  horizontal bar charts 73
  installing for Visual Studio, Python Tools
      used 66, 67
  installing, pip used 64, 65
  line chart, building 67-69
  scatter plots 77
  simple bar chart 71
  stacked bar charts 72
  stacked line charts 69
  URL 62
  XY charts 74
pygal charting library
  about 85
  URL 189
pygal style tool
  URL 126
pygal themes
  about 124-126
  URL 126
pygooglechart
  URL 190
pyramid charts 98-100
Python
  alternative shells 190
  basics 35-40
  HTTP, using in 132, 133
  installing, on Windows 9-14
  installing, URL 26
  JSON, parsing in 136-143
  JSONP, using with 144
  setting up, on Mac OS X 25-30
  setting up, on Ubuntu 31-34
  setting up, on Windows 7, 8
  XML, parsing in 134-136
Python 3
  URL 181

Python editors
  about 20-25
  IDE 20
Python Imaging Library. *See* PIL
Python modules
  about 160
  main method, building 161
Python Package Index (PyPi)
  about 8
  URL 9
Python Tools
  URL 190
  used, for installing pygal 66, 67
Python Tools installer
  URL 22
Pyvot
  about 186
  URL 186, 190
PyXLL
  URL 186, 190

R

radar charts 88
range() function 67
Really simple syndication. *See* RSS feed
Red Blue theme 125
replace() method 149
Rich Internet Applications (RIA) 136
RSS feed
  about 131
  modifying, for returning values 162, 163
  URL, for specification 131
RSS feed, modifying
  chart module, building 163
  chart, setting up for data 165, 166
  main function, configuring
    for passing data 167
  portable configuration, building
    for chart 164, 165

S

scatter plots 77, 78
SciPy stack
  URL 173
Snipplr, Python code
  URL 189

stacked bar charts 72
stacked line charts
  about 69
  building 69, 70
stacked pie charts 86, 87
Stack overflow, data visualizations
  URL 189
Stack overflow, Python questions
  URL 189
string format index
  %a 155
  %A 155
  %b 155
  %B 155
  %c 155
  %C 155
  %d 155
  %D 155
  %g 155
  %G 155
  %H 155
  %I 155
  %j 155
  %m 155
  %M 155
  %p 155
  %S 155
  %T 155
  %w 155
  %W 155
  %x 155
  %X 155
  %y 155
  %Y 156
  %z 156
  %Z 156
strptime
  using 150-154
strptime() method 150
struct_time object 152
Sublime Text
  URL 190
SVG graphics
  creating, svgwrite used 48
SVG graphics, creating with svgwrite
  for Eclipse, on Linux 50-58
  for Eclipse, on Mac 50-58

for Eclipse, on Windows 50
for editors, on Windows 50
for Windows users, with VSPT 48
svgwrite
URL 48
used, for creating SVG graphics 48

T

timedelta function 78

U

Ubuntu
Python, setting up on 31-34

V

values
returning, via RSS feed
modification 162, 163
Visual Studio
pygal, installing for 66, 67

W

Web
data, extracting from 127, 129
whisker plots. *See* **box plots**
Windows
Python installation, exploring 15-19
Python, installing on 9-14
Python, setting up 7, 8
Windows installer
URL 16
worldmap charts 101-103

X

x_label_rotation parameter 118
x_labels property 93
XML
about 130
parsing, in Python 134-136
URL, for specification 130
XPath
about 130
URL, for specification 130
XY charts
about 74
building 74-76

Z

zip() function 98

Thank you for buying
Learning Python Data Visualization

About Packt Publishing

Packt, pronounced 'packed', published its first book "*Mastering phpMyAdmin for Effective MySQL Management*" in April 2004 and subsequently continued to specialize in publishing highly focused books on specific technologies and solutions.

Our books and publications share the experiences of your fellow IT professionals in adapting and customizing today's systems, applications, and frameworks. Our solution based books give you the knowledge and power to customize the software and technologies you're using to get the job done. Packt books are more specific and less general than the IT books you have seen in the past. Our unique business model allows us to bring you more focused information, giving you more of what you need to know, and less of what you don't.

Packt is a modern, yet unique publishing company, which focuses on producing quality, cutting-edge books for communities of developers, administrators, and newbies alike. For more information, please visit our website: www.packtpub.com.

About Packt Open Source

In 2010, Packt launched two new brands, Packt Open Source and Packt Enterprise, in order to continue its focus on specialization. This book is part of the Packt Open Source brand, home to books published on software built around Open Source licenses, and offering information to anybody from advanced developers to budding web designers. The Open Source brand also runs Packt's Open Source Royalty Scheme, by which Packt gives a royalty to each Open Source project about whose software a book is sold.

Writing for Packt

We welcome all inquiries from people who are interested in authoring. Book proposals should be sent to author@packtpub.com. If your book idea is still at an early stage and you would like to discuss it first before writing a formal book proposal, contact us; one of our commissioning editors will get in touch with you.

We're not just looking for published authors; if you have strong technical skills but no writing experience, our experienced editors can help you develop a writing career, or simply get some additional reward for your expertise.

Python High Performance Programming

ISBN: 978-1-78328-845-8   Paperback: 108 pages

Boost the performance of your Python programs using advanced techniques

1. Identify the bottlenecks in your applications and solve them using the best profiling techniques.

2. Write efficient numerical code in NumPy and Cython.

3. Adapt your programs to run on multiple processors with parallel programming.

Python Data Visualization Cookbook

ISBN: 978-1-78216-336-7   Paperback: 280 pages

Over 60 recipes that will enable you to learn how to create attractive visualizations using Python's most popular libraries

1. Learn how to set up an optimal Python environment for data visualization.

2. Understand the topics such as importing data for visualization and formatting data for visualization.

3. Understand the underlying data and how to use the right visualizations.

Please check **www.PacktPub.com** for information on our titles

**Learning IPython for Interactive
Computing and Data Visualization**

ISBN: 978-1-78216-993-2   Paperback: 138 pages

Learn IPython for interactive Python programming,
high-performance numerical computing, and
data visualization

1. A practical step-by-step tutorial which will
    help you to replace the Python console with the
    powerful IPython command-line interface.

2. Use the IPython notebook to modernize the way
    you interact with Python.

3. Perform highly efficient computations with
    NumPy and Pandas.

Matplotlib for Python Developers

ISBN: 978-1-84719-790-0   Paperback: 308 pages

Build remarkable publication-quality plots the
easy way

1. Create high quality 2D plots by using
    matplotlib productively.

2. Incremental introduction to matplotlib, from
    the ground up to advanced levels.

3. Embed matplotlib in GTK+, Qt, and wxWidgets
    applications as well as websites to utilize them
    in Python applications.

4. Deploy matplotlib in web applications and
    expose it on the Web using popular web
    frameworks such as Pylons and Django.

Please check **www.PacktPub.com** for information on our titles